50 South Korean Bread Making Recipes for Home

By: Kelly Johnson

Table of Contents

- Hotteok (호떡): Sweet Korean pancakes filled with a mixture of brown sugar, cinnamon, and chopped nuts.
- Gyeranppang (계란빵): Fluffy bread rolls with a whole egg baked into the center.
- Soboro Bread (소보로빵): Soft bread topped with a crumbly streusel made from flour, sugar, and butter.
- Chapssal Donuts (찹쌀도넛): Korean-style donuts made with glutinous rice flour, giving them a chewy texture.
- Cream Cheese Bread (크림치즈빵): Soft and fluffy bread rolls filled with sweet cream cheese filling.
- Korean Melon Bread (메론빵): Sweet bread rolls with a crispy cookie crust on top, resembling a melon.
- Red Bean Bun (팥빵): Soft bread rolls filled with sweet red bean paste.
- Sweet Potato Bread (고구마빵): Bread made with mashed sweet potatoes, adding natural sweetness and moisture.
- Green Tea Bread (녹차빵): Bread flavored with matcha green tea powder, giving it a unique color and flavor.
- Hodugwaja (호두과자): Walnut-shaped bread filled with sweet red bean paste and walnuts, a popular Korean street food snack.
- Hwangnam Bread (황남빵): Sweet bread filled with red bean paste and covered in a crispy cookie crust.
- Sesame Seed Bread (참깨빵): Bread topped with toasted sesame seeds for a nutty flavor and crunchy texture.
- Chestnut Bread (밤빵): Bread made with pureed chestnuts for a sweet and earthy flavor.
- Potato Bread (감자빵): Soft bread made with mashed potatoes, adding moisture and a slightly sweet taste.
- Sausage Bread (소세지빵): Bread rolls stuffed with savory sausage pieces.
- Apple Cinnamon Bread (사과 시나몬빵): Bread infused with apple chunks and cinnamon for a fragrant and sweet flavor.
- Green Onion Bread (파빵): Bread rolls filled with chopped green onions, adding a savory twist to the bread.
- Sweet Red Bean Bun (찐빵): Steamed buns filled with sweet red bean paste, a classic Korean dessert.

- Corn Bread (옥수수빵): Bread made with cornmeal and sweet corn kernels, offering a slightly sweet and crunchy texture.
- Cinnamon Raisin Bread (시나몬 레이즌빵): Bread flavored with cinnamon and studded with plump raisins for a sweet and aromatic treat.
- Kimchi Bread (김치빵): Savory bread rolls filled with spicy and tangy kimchi, perfect for a unique flavor twist.
- Seaweed Bread (김빵): Bread rolls filled with dried seaweed flakes, adding a salty and umami-rich taste.
- Chocolate Croissant (초콜릿 크로아상): Buttery croissants filled with rich chocolate, perfect for a decadent breakfast or snack.
- Custard Cream Bun (크림빵): Soft bread rolls filled with creamy custard filling, a beloved Korean bakery staple.
- Rice Cake Bread (떡빵): Bread rolls stuffed with sweet and chewy rice cakes, offering a delightful combination of textures.
- Sweet Potato Cream Bread (고구마 크림빵): Bread filled with a creamy sweet potato filling, offering a comforting and indulgent treat.
- Honey Butter Bread (꿀버터빵): Soft bread rolls coated in a sweet and buttery honey glaze, perfect for a sweet and indulgent snack.
- Cheese Bread (치즈빵): Soft bread rolls filled with gooey melted cheese, offering a savory and satisfying flavor.
- Almond Cream Bread (아몬드 크림빵): Bread rolls filled with creamy almond paste, topped with sliced almonds for a crunchy texture.
- Caramel Bread (카라멜빵): Bread rolls drizzled with rich caramel sauce, offering a sweet and indulgent flavor.
- Black Sesame Bread (검은깨빵): Bread rolls infused with ground black sesame seeds for a nutty flavor and striking color.
- Sweet Red Bean Roll (팥 롤빵): Soft bread rolls filled with sweet red bean paste and rolled into a log shape.
- Cream Corn Bread (크림 옥수수빵): Bread rolls filled with creamy sweet corn filling, offering a sweet and savory flavor profile.
- Sweet Potato Walnut Bread (고구마 호두빵): Bread made with mashed sweet potatoes and studded with chopped walnuts for added texture and flavor.
- Cinnamon Sugar Breadsticks (시나몬 슈가 브레드스틱): Crispy breadsticks coated in cinnamon sugar, perfect for a sweet and crunchy snack.
- Potato Bacon Bread (감자 베이컨빵): Bread rolls filled with mashed potatoes and crispy bacon pieces, offering a savory and satisfying flavor combination.

- **Cheese Onion Bread (치즈 양파빵)**: Bread rolls filled with melted cheese and caramelized onions, offering a rich and savory taste.
- **Matcha Red Bean Bun (녹차 팥빵)**: Soft bread rolls infused with matcha green tea powder and filled with sweet red bean paste.
- **Apple Walnut Bread (사과 호두빵)**: Bread rolls filled with diced apples and chopped walnuts, offering a sweet and nutty flavor.
- **Pumpkin Bread (호박빵)**: Bread made with pureed pumpkin for a moist and flavorful texture, perfect for autumn baking.
- **Sweet Red Bean Milk Bread (팥빵)**: Soft and fluffy milk bread filled with sweet red bean paste, a classic Korean bakery treat.
- **Cream Cheese Walnut Bread (크림치즈 호두빵)**: Bread rolls filled with creamy cheese and crunchy walnuts, offering a delightful combination of flavors and textures.
- **Honey Almond Bread (꿀 아몬드빵)**: Bread rolls drizzled with honey and topped with sliced almonds, offering a sweet and nutty flavor.
- **Green Tea Red Bean Bread (녹차 팥빵)**: Bread rolls infused with green tea flavor and filled with sweet red bean paste, offering a unique and delicious taste.
- **Sweet Potato Chestnut Bread (고구마 밤빵)**: Bread made with mashed sweet potatoes and studded with chestnuts, offering a sweet and nutty flavor profile.
- **Sesame Seed Sweet Bread (참깨 단빵)**: Sweet bread rolls coated with sesame seeds for a nutty flavor and crunchy texture.
- **Cream Corn Milk Bread (크림 옥수수우유빵)**: Soft milk bread rolls filled with creamy sweet corn filling, offering a sweet and comforting taste.
- **Chocolate Cream Bread (초콜릿 크림빵)**: Soft bread rolls filled with rich chocolate cream filling, perfect for chocolate lovers.
- **Green Onion Cheese Bread (파 치즈빵)**: Bread rolls filled with melted cheese and chopped green onions, offering a savory and flavorful taste.
- **Sweet Red Bean Twist Bread (팥빵)**: Twisted bread rolls filled with sweet red bean paste, offering a fun and delicious treat.

Hotteok (호떡): Sweet Korean pancakes filled with a mixture of brown sugar, cinnamon, and chopped nuts.

Ingredients:

For the Dough:

- 2 cups all-purpose flour
- 1 cup lukewarm water
- 1 tablespoon sugar
- 1 teaspoon active dry yeast
- 1/2 teaspoon salt

For the Filling:

- 1/2 cup brown sugar
- 1 teaspoon cinnamon
- 1/4 cup chopped nuts (such as walnuts or peanuts)
- Optional: 1 tablespoon honey or maple syrup

For Frying:

- Vegetable oil for frying

Instructions:

1. In a mixing bowl, combine the lukewarm water, sugar, and active dry yeast. Let it sit for about 5-10 minutes until the yeast activates and becomes frothy.
2. In a separate bowl, sift the flour and salt together. Gradually add the flour mixture to the yeast mixture, stirring until a dough forms.
3. Knead the dough on a lightly floured surface for about 5-7 minutes until it becomes smooth and elastic. Place the dough in a greased bowl, cover it with a clean kitchen towel, and let it rise in a warm place for about 1-2 hours until it doubles in size.
4. While the dough is rising, prepare the filling. In a small bowl, mix together the brown sugar, cinnamon, chopped nuts, and honey or maple syrup (if using). Set aside.

5. Once the dough has risen, punch it down and divide it into equal-sized balls, about the size of golf balls.
6. Take one dough ball and flatten it into a small disk with your fingers. Place a spoonful of the filling mixture in the center of the dough disk.
7. Carefully gather the edges of the dough around the filling and pinch them together to seal, forming a ball shape. Make sure the filling is completely enclosed within the dough.
8. Flatten the filled dough ball slightly with your palm to form a pancake shape, about 1/2 inch thick.
9. Heat a frying pan over medium heat and add enough vegetable oil to cover the bottom of the pan.
10. Place the filled dough ball in the pan and flatten it gently with a spatula to form a pancake shape. Cook for 2-3 minutes until the bottom is golden brown.
11. Carefully flip the pancake and cook for another 2-3 minutes until the other side is golden brown and the filling is melted and gooey.
12. Remove the Hotteok from the pan and drain on paper towels. Repeat the process with the remaining dough balls and filling.
13. Serve the Hotteok warm and enjoy the delicious, sweet, and satisfying treat!

Feel free to adjust the filling ingredients according to your preference. You can also experiment with different fillings such as Nutella, sweetened condensed milk, or cheese.

Gyeranppang (계란빵): Fluffy bread rolls with a whole egg baked into the center.

Ingredients:

- 2 cups all-purpose flour
- 1 cup lukewarm milk
- 1/4 cup sugar
- 2 1/4 teaspoons active dry yeast
- 1/4 cup unsalted butter, melted
- 1 teaspoon salt
- 6 large eggs, at room temperature
- Cooking spray or butter for greasing the pan

Instructions:

1. In a small bowl, combine the lukewarm milk, sugar, and active dry yeast. Let it sit for about 5-10 minutes until the yeast activates and becomes frothy.
2. In a large mixing bowl, combine the flour and salt. Gradually add the yeast mixture and melted butter to the flour mixture, stirring until a dough forms.
3. Knead the dough on a lightly floured surface for about 5-7 minutes until it becomes smooth and elastic. Place the dough in a greased bowl, cover it with a clean kitchen towel, and let it rise in a warm place for about 1-2 hours until it doubles in size.
4. Once the dough has risen, punch it down and divide it into 6 equal-sized balls.
5. Roll each dough ball into a flat circle, about 1/4 inch thick. Place a whole egg in the center of each dough circle.
6. Carefully fold the edges of the dough up and around the egg, pinching them together to seal and form a ball shape.
7. Place the filled dough balls seam side down in a greased muffin tin or on a baking sheet lined with parchment paper. Cover them loosely with a clean kitchen towel and let them rise for another 30-45 minutes.
8. Preheat your oven to 350°F (175°C).
9. Once the dough balls have risen again, brush the tops lightly with beaten egg for a shiny finish (optional).
10. Bake the Gyeranppang in the preheated oven for 15-20 minutes until they are golden brown and the eggs are cooked to your desired level of doneness.
11. Remove the Gyeranppang from the oven and let them cool slightly before serving.

12. Enjoy your homemade Gyeranppang warm as a delicious and comforting snack or breakfast treat!

Feel free to experiment with different fillings or toppings for your Gyeranppang, such as cheese, bacon, or herbs.

Soboro Bread (소보로빵): Soft bread topped with a crumbly streusel made from flour, sugar, and butter.

Ingredients:

For the Bread:

- 2 cups all-purpose flour
- 1/4 cup granulated sugar
- 1 tablespoon instant yeast
- 1/2 teaspoon salt
- 1/2 cup warm milk
- 1/4 cup unsalted butter, melted
- 1 large egg

For the Streusel Topping:

- 1/2 cup all-purpose flour
- 1/4 cup granulated sugar
- 1/4 cup unsalted butter, cold

Instructions:

1. In a large mixing bowl, combine the flour, sugar, instant yeast, and salt.
2. In a separate bowl, whisk together the warm milk, melted butter, and egg.
3. Pour the wet ingredients into the dry ingredients and mix until a dough forms.
4. Knead the dough on a lightly floured surface for about 5-7 minutes until it becomes smooth and elastic.
5. Place the dough in a greased bowl, cover it with a clean kitchen towel, and let it rise in a warm place for about 1-2 hours until it doubles in size.
6. Once the dough has risen, punch it down and divide it into equal-sized balls, about the size of golf balls.
7. Place the dough balls on a baking sheet lined with parchment paper, leaving some space between each one.
8. To make the streusel topping, combine the flour and sugar in a bowl. Cut in the cold butter using a pastry cutter or your fingers until the mixture resembles coarse crumbs.

9. Sprinkle the streusel topping evenly over the dough balls.
10. Preheat your oven to 350°F (175°C).
11. Bake the Soboro bread in the preheated oven for 15-20 minutes until they are golden brown and cooked through.
12. Remove the bread from the oven and let them cool slightly before serving.
13. Enjoy your homemade Soboro bread as a delicious sweet treat with a cup of coffee or tea!

Feel free to customize your Soboro bread by adding flavors such as cinnamon or vanilla to the dough or using different types of streusel toppings.

Chapssal Donuts (찹쌀도넛): Korean-style donuts made with glutinous rice flour, giving them a chewy texture.

Ingredients:

For the Doughnuts:

- 1 cup glutinous rice flour (chapssalgaru)
- 1/4 cup all-purpose flour
- 1/4 cup granulated sugar
- 1/2 teaspoon baking powder
- Pinch of salt
- 1/4 cup milk
- 1 tablespoon melted butter
- 1 teaspoon vanilla extract
- Vegetable oil for frying

For the Coating (Optional):

- Granulated sugar
- Cinnamon (optional)

Instructions:

1. In a mixing bowl, combine the glutinous rice flour, all-purpose flour, sugar, baking powder, and salt.
2. Add the milk, melted butter, and vanilla extract to the dry ingredients. Mix until a smooth dough forms. If the dough is too dry, you can add a little more milk, 1 tablespoon at a time, until it comes together.
3. Cover the dough with plastic wrap and let it rest for about 15-20 minutes.
4. After resting, divide the dough into small portions and roll each portion into a ball. Then, flatten each ball slightly to form a donut shape. You can use a donut cutter or simply use your hands.
5. Heat vegetable oil in a deep fryer or heavy-bottomed pot to 350°F (175°C).

6. Carefully add the doughnuts to the hot oil, a few at a time, making sure not to overcrowd the pot. Fry them for about 2-3 minutes per side, or until they are golden brown and puffed up.
7. Once cooked, remove the doughnuts from the oil using a slotted spoon and drain them on paper towels to remove excess oil.
8. If desired, coat the warm doughnuts in granulated sugar or a mixture of sugar and cinnamon while they are still slightly warm.
9. Serve the Chapssal Donuts warm and enjoy their delicious chewy texture!

These Chapssal Donuts are best enjoyed fresh, but you can store any leftovers in an airtight container at room temperature for up to 2 days. Simply reheat them in the oven or microwave before serving. Enjoy!

Cream Cheese Bread (크림치즈빵): Soft and fluffy bread rolls filled with sweet cream cheese filling.

Ingredients:

For the Bread Dough:

- 2 cups all-purpose flour
- 1/4 cup granulated sugar
- 1 teaspoon instant yeast
- 1/2 teaspoon salt
- 3/4 cup warm milk
- 1/4 cup unsalted butter, melted
- 1 large egg

For the Cream Cheese Filling:

- 8 oz cream cheese, softened
- 1/4 cup granulated sugar
- 1 teaspoon vanilla extract

For the Egg Wash (Optional):

- 1 egg, beaten

Instructions:

1. In a large mixing bowl, combine the flour, sugar, instant yeast, and salt.
2. In a separate bowl, whisk together the warm milk, melted butter, and egg.
3. Pour the wet ingredients into the dry ingredients and mix until a dough forms.
4. Knead the dough on a lightly floured surface for about 5-7 minutes until it becomes smooth and elastic.
5. Place the dough in a greased bowl, cover it with a clean kitchen towel, and let it rise in a warm place for about 1-2 hours until it doubles in size.

6. While the dough is rising, prepare the cream cheese filling. In a mixing bowl, beat the softened cream cheese, sugar, and vanilla extract until smooth and creamy. Set aside.
7. Once the dough has risen, punch it down and divide it into equal-sized portions.
8. Flatten each dough portion into a small circle. Place a spoonful of the cream cheese filling in the center of each dough circle.
9. Carefully gather the edges of the dough up and around the cream cheese filling, pinching them together to seal.
10. Place the filled dough balls seam side down on a baking sheet lined with parchment paper, leaving some space between each one.
11. Cover the dough balls loosely with a clean kitchen towel and let them rise for another 30-45 minutes.
12. Preheat your oven to 350°F (175°C).
13. If using, brush the risen dough balls with beaten egg for a shiny finish.
14. Bake the Cream Cheese Bread in the preheated oven for 15-20 minutes until they are golden brown and cooked through.
15. Remove the bread from the oven and let them cool slightly before serving.
16. Enjoy your homemade Cream Cheese Bread warm as a delicious and indulgent treat!

Feel free to adjust the sweetness of the cream cheese filling to your preference by adding more or less sugar. You can also experiment with adding other flavorings such as lemon zest or cinnamon for added depth of flavor.

Korean Melon Bread (메론빵): Sweet bread rolls with a crispy cookie crust on top, resembling a melon.

Ingredients:

For the Bread Dough:

- 2 cups all-purpose flour
- 1/4 cup granulated sugar
- 1 teaspoon instant yeast
- 1/2 teaspoon salt
- 3/4 cup warm milk
- 1/4 cup unsalted butter, melted
- 1 large egg

For the Cookie Crust:

- 1/4 cup unsalted butter, softened
- 1/4 cup granulated sugar
- 1/2 cup all-purpose flour
- 1/4 teaspoon baking powder
- A few drops of green food coloring (optional)
- Chocolate chips or raisins for decoration (optional)

Instructions:

1. In a large mixing bowl, combine the flour, sugar, instant yeast, and salt.
2. In a separate bowl, whisk together the warm milk, melted butter, and egg.
3. Pour the wet ingredients into the dry ingredients and mix until a dough forms.
4. Knead the dough on a lightly floured surface for about 5-7 minutes until it becomes smooth and elastic.
5. Place the dough in a greased bowl, cover it with a clean kitchen towel, and let it rise in a warm place for about 1-2 hours until it doubles in size.
6. While the dough is rising, prepare the cookie crust. In a mixing bowl, cream together the softened butter and sugar until light and fluffy. Add the flour and

baking powder, and mix until crumbly. Add a few drops of green food coloring if desired, and mix until the color is evenly distributed.
7. Once the dough has risen, punch it down and divide it into equal-sized portions.
8. Shape each dough portion into a ball and place them on a baking sheet lined with parchment paper, leaving some space between each one.
9. Flatten each dough ball slightly with your palm.
10. Divide the cookie crust mixture into equal-sized portions and flatten them into discs that are slightly larger than the dough balls.
11. Place a cookie crust disc on top of each dough ball, pressing down gently to adhere.
12. Use a knife or a toothpick to create a crisscross pattern on the surface of the cookie crust to resemble the texture of a melon.
13. If desired, decorate the surface of each bread roll with chocolate chips or raisins to resemble melon seeds.
14. Preheat your oven to 350°F (175°C).
15. Bake the Korean Melon Bread in the preheated oven for 15-20 minutes until the cookie crust is golden brown and crispy.
16. Remove the bread from the oven and let them cool slightly before serving.
17. Enjoy your homemade Korean Melon Bread warm as a delicious and whimsical treat!

Feel free to adjust the sweetness of the bread dough and cookie crust according to your preference. You can also experiment with different flavors and colors for the cookie crust to create variations of Korean Melon Bread.

Red Bean Bun (팥빵): Soft bread rolls filled with sweet red bean paste.

Ingredients:

For the Dough:

- 2 cups all-purpose flour
- 1/4 cup granulated sugar
- 1 teaspoon instant yeast
- 1/2 teaspoon salt
- 3/4 cup warm milk
- 1/4 cup unsalted butter, melted
- 1 large egg

For the Red Bean Filling:

- 1 cup sweetened red bean paste (store-bought or homemade)

Instructions:

1. In a large mixing bowl, combine the flour, sugar, instant yeast, and salt.
2. In a separate bowl, whisk together the warm milk, melted butter, and egg.
3. Pour the wet ingredients into the dry ingredients and mix until a dough forms.
4. Knead the dough on a lightly floured surface for about 5-7 minutes until it becomes smooth and elastic.
5. Place the dough in a greased bowl, cover it with a clean kitchen towel, and let it rise in a warm place for about 1-2 hours until it doubles in size.
6. Once the dough has risen, punch it down and divide it into equal-sized portions.
7. Take one portion of dough and flatten it into a small circle with your hands or a rolling pin.
8. Place a spoonful of sweetened red bean paste in the center of the dough circle.
9. Carefully gather the edges of the dough up and around the red bean paste, pinching them together to seal and form a bun shape.
10. Repeat the process with the remaining dough and red bean paste.

11. Place the filled buns seam side down on a baking sheet lined with parchment paper, leaving some space between each one.
12. Cover the buns loosely with a clean kitchen towel and let them rise for another 30-45 minutes.
13. Preheat your oven to 350°F (175°C).
14. Once the buns have risen, bake them in the preheated oven for 15-20 minutes until they are golden brown and cooked through.
15. Remove the Red Bean Buns from the oven and let them cool slightly before serving.
16. Enjoy your homemade Red Bean Buns warm as a delicious and comforting treat!

Feel free to adjust the sweetness of the red bean paste filling to your preference. You can also add a sprinkle of sesame seeds on top of the buns before baking for added flavor and texture.

Sweet Potato Bread (고구마빵): Bread made with mashed sweet potatoes, adding natural sweetness and moisture.

Ingredients:

- 1 cup mashed sweet potatoes (about 2 medium-sized sweet potatoes)
- 2 cups all-purpose flour
- 1/4 cup granulated sugar
- 1 teaspoon instant yeast
- 1/2 teaspoon salt
- 1/2 cup warm milk
- 1/4 cup unsalted butter, melted
- 1 large egg

Instructions:

1. Preheat your oven to 350°F (175°C). Grease a loaf pan or line it with parchment paper.
2. Cook the sweet potatoes: Wash the sweet potatoes and prick them with a fork. Microwave them on high for 5-7 minutes until they are soft and fully cooked. Alternatively, you can bake them in the oven at 400°F (200°C) for 45-60 minutes. Let them cool slightly, then peel and mash them until smooth. Measure out 1 cup of mashed sweet potatoes for the recipe.
3. In a large mixing bowl, combine the mashed sweet potatoes, flour, sugar, instant yeast, and salt.
4. In a separate bowl, whisk together the warm milk, melted butter, and egg.
5. Pour the wet ingredients into the dry ingredients and mix until a dough forms.
6. Knead the dough on a lightly floured surface for about 5-7 minutes until it becomes smooth and elastic.
7. Place the dough in a greased bowl, cover it with a clean kitchen towel, and let it rise in a warm place for about 1-2 hours until it doubles in size.
8. Once the dough has risen, punch it down and shape it into a loaf. Place the loaf in the prepared loaf pan.
9. Cover the loaf loosely with a clean kitchen towel and let it rise for another 30-45 minutes.
10. Bake the Sweet Potato Bread in the preheated oven for 30-35 minutes until it is golden brown and sounds hollow when tapped on the bottom.

11. Remove the bread from the oven and let it cool in the pan for a few minutes before transferring it to a wire rack to cool completely.
12. Once cooled, slice and serve the Sweet Potato Bread. Enjoy it plain or with butter or your favorite spread.

Feel free to customize this recipe by adding spices like cinnamon or nutmeg for extra flavor. You can also add chopped nuts or dried fruits for texture and variety.

Green Tea Bread (녹차빵): Bread flavored with matcha green tea powder, giving it a unique color and flavor.

Ingredients:

- 2 cups all-purpose flour
- 1/4 cup granulated sugar
- 1 tablespoon matcha green tea powder
- 1 teaspoon instant yeast
- 1/2 teaspoon salt
- 3/4 cup warm milk
- 1/4 cup unsalted butter, melted
- 1 large egg

Instructions:

1. Preheat your oven to 350°F (175°C). Grease a loaf pan or line it with parchment paper.
2. In a large mixing bowl, sift together the flour, sugar, matcha green tea powder, instant yeast, and salt.
3. In a separate bowl, whisk together the warm milk, melted butter, and egg.
4. Pour the wet ingredients into the dry ingredients and mix until a dough forms.
5. Knead the dough on a lightly floured surface for about 5-7 minutes until it becomes smooth and elastic.
6. Place the dough in a greased bowl, cover it with a clean kitchen towel, and let it rise in a warm place for about 1-2 hours until it doubles in size.
7. Once the dough has risen, punch it down and shape it into a loaf. Place the loaf in the prepared loaf pan.
8. Cover the loaf loosely with a clean kitchen towel and let it rise for another 30-45 minutes.
9. Bake the Green Tea Bread in the preheated oven for 30-35 minutes until it is golden brown and sounds hollow when tapped on the bottom.
10. Remove the bread from the oven and let it cool in the pan for a few minutes before transferring it to a wire rack to cool completely.
11. Once cooled, slice and serve the Green Tea Bread. Enjoy it plain or with butter or your favorite spread.

Feel free to customize this recipe by adjusting the amount of matcha green tea powder to your preference. You can also add ingredients like chopped nuts or white chocolate chips for extra flavor and texture.

Hodugwaja (호두과자): Walnut-shaped bread filled with sweet red bean paste and walnuts, a popular Korean street food snack.

Ingredients:

For the Dough:

- 1 cup all-purpose flour
- 1/4 cup glutinous rice flour
- 1/4 cup granulated sugar
- 1/4 teaspoon salt
- 1/2 teaspoon instant yeast
- 1/2 cup warm milk
- 2 tablespoons unsalted butter, melted
- 1 large egg, beaten

For the Filling:

- 1/2 cup sweetened red bean paste (store-bought or homemade)
- 1/4 cup chopped walnuts

For the Mold:

- Hodugwaja mold (available online or in Korean specialty stores)

Instructions:

1. In a large mixing bowl, combine the all-purpose flour, glutinous rice flour, sugar, salt, and instant yeast.
2. Add the warm milk, melted butter, and beaten egg to the dry ingredients. Mix until a dough forms.
3. Knead the dough on a lightly floured surface for about 5-7 minutes until it becomes smooth and elastic.

4. Place the dough in a greased bowl, cover it with a clean kitchen towel, and let it rise in a warm place for about 1-2 hours until it doubles in size.
5. Once the dough has risen, punch it down and divide it into equal-sized portions.
6. Take one portion of dough and flatten it into a small circle with your hands or a rolling pin.
7. Place a small amount of sweetened red bean paste and chopped walnuts in the center of the dough circle.
8. Carefully gather the edges of the dough up and around the filling, pinching them together to seal and form a walnut shape.
9. Repeat the process with the remaining dough and filling.
10. Preheat your oven to 350°F (175°C). Place the hodugwaja mold on a baking sheet lined with parchment paper.
11. Place each filled hodugwaja into the mold, pressing down gently to shape it.
12. Bake the hodugwaja in the preheated oven for 15-20 minutes until they are golden brown and cooked through.
13. Remove the hodugwaja from the oven and let them cool slightly before serving.
14. Enjoy your homemade hodugwaja warm as a delicious and nostalgic Korean street food snack!

Feel free to experiment with different fillings for your hodugwaja, such as sweetened chestnut paste or a combination of red bean paste and nuts. You can also add a sprinkle of sesame seeds on top for extra flavor and texture.

Hwangnam Bread (황남빵): Sweet bread filled with red bean paste and covered in a crispy cookie crust.

Ingredients:

For the Bread Dough:

- 2 cups all-purpose flour
- 1/4 cup granulated sugar
- 1 teaspoon instant yeast
- 1/2 teaspoon salt
- 3/4 cup warm milk
- 1/4 cup unsalted butter, melted
- 1 large egg

For the Red Bean Filling:

- 1 cup sweetened red bean paste (store-bought or homemade)

For the Cookie Crust:

- 1/4 cup unsalted butter, softened
- 1/4 cup granulated sugar
- 1/2 cup all-purpose flour
- 1/4 teaspoon baking powder

Instructions:

1. Preheat your oven to 350°F (175°C). Grease a baking sheet or line it with parchment paper.
2. In a large mixing bowl, combine the flour, sugar, instant yeast, and salt.
3. In a separate bowl, whisk together the warm milk, melted butter, and egg.
4. Pour the wet ingredients into the dry ingredients and mix until a dough forms.

5. Knead the dough on a lightly floured surface for about 5-7 minutes until it becomes smooth and elastic.
6. Divide the dough into equal-sized portions, depending on how large you want your Hwangnam Bread to be.
7. Flatten each dough portion into a small circle with your hands.
8. Place a spoonful of sweetened red bean paste in the center of each dough circle.
9. Carefully gather the edges of the dough up and around the red bean paste, pinching them together to seal.
10. In a mixing bowl, cream together the softened butter and sugar for the cookie crust until light and fluffy.
11. Add the flour and baking powder to the butter mixture, and mix until crumbly.
12. Take a portion of the cookie crust mixture and flatten it into a disc slightly larger than the filled dough.
13. Place the filled dough on top of the cookie crust disc.
14. Gather the edges of the cookie crust up and around the filled dough, covering it completely. Press down gently to adhere.
15. Repeat the process with the remaining dough and filling.
16. Place the assembled Hwangnam Breads on the prepared baking sheet.
17. Bake in the preheated oven for 20-25 minutes until the cookie crust is golden brown and crispy.
18. Remove from the oven and let cool slightly before serving.
19. Enjoy your homemade Hwangnam Bread warm as a delicious and comforting treat!

Feel free to adjust the sweetness of the red bean paste to your preference. You can also add chopped nuts or dried fruits to the filling for extra flavor and texture.

Sesame Seed Bread (참깨빵): Bread topped with toasted sesame seeds for a nutty flavor and crunchy texture.

Ingredients:

- 2 cups all-purpose flour
- 1/4 cup granulated sugar
- 1 teaspoon instant yeast
- 1/2 teaspoon salt
- 3/4 cup warm milk
- 1/4 cup unsalted butter, melted
- 1 large egg
- 1/4 cup toasted sesame seeds

Instructions:

1. Preheat your oven to 350°F (175°C). Grease a loaf pan or line it with parchment paper.
2. In a large mixing bowl, combine the flour, sugar, instant yeast, and salt.
3. In a separate bowl, whisk together the warm milk, melted butter, and egg.
4. Pour the wet ingredients into the dry ingredients and mix until a dough forms.
5. Knead the dough on a lightly floured surface for about 5-7 minutes until it becomes smooth and elastic.
6. Place the dough in a greased bowl, cover it with a clean kitchen towel, and let it rise in a warm place for about 1-2 hours until it doubles in size.
7. Once the dough has risen, punch it down and shape it into a loaf. Place the loaf in the prepared loaf pan.
8. Cover the loaf loosely with a clean kitchen towel and let it rise for another 30-45 minutes.
9. Brush the top of the loaf with a little milk and sprinkle the toasted sesame seeds evenly over the surface.
10. Bake the Sesame Seed Bread in the preheated oven for 30-35 minutes until it is golden brown and sounds hollow when tapped on the bottom.
11. Remove the bread from the oven and let it cool in the pan for a few minutes before transferring it to a wire rack to cool completely.
12. Once cooled, slice and serve the Sesame Seed Bread. Enjoy it plain or with butter or your favorite spread.

Feel free to experiment with different types of seeds or nuts for variation. You can also add a tablespoon of honey to the dough for a touch of sweetness.

Chestnut Bread (밤빵): Bread made with pureed chestnuts for a sweet and earthy flavor.

Ingredients:

- 2 cups all-purpose flour
- 1/4 cup granulated sugar
- 1 teaspoon instant yeast
- 1/2 teaspoon salt
- 3/4 cup warm milk
- 1/4 cup unsalted butter, melted
- 1 large egg
- 1 cup chestnut puree (store-bought or homemade)

Instructions:

1. Preheat your oven to 350°F (175°C). Grease a loaf pan or line it with parchment paper.
2. In a large mixing bowl, combine the flour, sugar, instant yeast, and salt.
3. In a separate bowl, whisk together the warm milk, melted butter, and egg.
4. Pour the wet ingredients into the dry ingredients and mix until a dough forms.
5. Knead the dough on a lightly floured surface for about 5-7 minutes until it becomes smooth and elastic.
6. Place the dough in a greased bowl, cover it with a clean kitchen towel, and let it rise in a warm place for about 1-2 hours until it doubles in size.
7. Once the dough has risen, punch it down and shape it into a loaf. Place the loaf in the prepared loaf pan.
8. Cover the loaf loosely with a clean kitchen towel and let it rise for another 30-45 minutes.
9. While the dough is rising, prepare the chestnut puree. If using fresh chestnuts, peel and boil them until soft, then puree them in a food processor until smooth. If using store-bought chestnut puree, simply measure out 1 cup.
10. Once the dough has risen, make a shallow indentation down the center of the loaf using the back of a spoon or your fingers.
11. Spoon the chestnut puree into the indentation, spreading it evenly along the length of the loaf.
12. Bake the Chestnut Bread in the preheated oven for 30-35 minutes until it is golden brown and sounds hollow when tapped on the bottom.

13. Remove the bread from the oven and let it cool in the pan for a few minutes before transferring it to a wire rack to cool completely.
14. Once cooled, slice and serve the Chestnut Bread. Enjoy it plain or with butter or your favorite spread.

Feel free to add a sprinkle of cinnamon or nutmeg to the dough for extra flavor. You can also add chopped nuts or dried fruits to the bread for added texture and variety.

Potato Bread (감자빵): Soft bread made with mashed potatoes, adding moisture and a slightly sweet taste.

Ingredients:

- 1 cup mashed potatoes (about 2 medium-sized potatoes)
- 2 cups all-purpose flour
- 1/4 cup granulated sugar
- 1 teaspoon instant yeast
- 1/2 teaspoon salt
- 3/4 cup warm milk
- 1/4 cup unsalted butter, melted
- 1 large egg

Instructions:

1. Preheat your oven to 350°F (175°C). Grease a loaf pan or line it with parchment paper.
2. Peel the potatoes and cut them into small chunks. Boil the potatoes in a pot of water until they are fork-tender, about 15-20 minutes. Drain the potatoes and mash them until smooth. Measure out 1 cup of mashed potatoes for the recipe.
3. In a large mixing bowl, combine the mashed potatoes, flour, sugar, instant yeast, and salt.
4. In a separate bowl, whisk together the warm milk, melted butter, and egg.
5. Pour the wet ingredients into the dry ingredients and mix until a dough forms.
6. Knead the dough on a lightly floured surface for about 5-7 minutes until it becomes smooth and elastic.
7. Place the dough in a greased bowl, cover it with a clean kitchen towel, and let it rise in a warm place for about 1-2 hours until it doubles in size.
8. Once the dough has risen, punch it down and shape it into a loaf. Place the loaf in the prepared loaf pan.
9. Cover the loaf loosely with a clean kitchen towel and let it rise for another 30-45 minutes.
10. Bake the Potato Bread in the preheated oven for 30-35 minutes until it is golden brown and sounds hollow when tapped on the bottom.
11. Remove the bread from the oven and let it cool in the pan for a few minutes before transferring it to a wire rack to cool completely.

12. Once cooled, slice and serve the Potato Bread. Enjoy it plain or with butter or your favorite spread.

Feel free to add herbs or spices like rosemary, garlic powder, or black pepper to the dough for extra flavor. You can also sprinkle some grated cheese on top of the loaf before baking for a cheesy twist.

Sausage Bread (소세지빵): Bread rolls stuffed with savory sausage pieces.

Ingredients:

For the Bread Dough:

- 3 cups all-purpose flour
- 1/4 cup granulated sugar
- 1 teaspoon salt
- 2 teaspoons instant yeast
- 1 cup warm milk
- 1/4 cup unsalted butter, melted
- 1 large egg

For the Sausage Filling:

- 6-8 sausages, cooked and chopped into small pieces
- 1 cup shredded cheese (optional)

Instructions:

1. In a large mixing bowl, combine the flour, sugar, salt, and instant yeast.
2. In a separate bowl, whisk together the warm milk, melted butter, and egg.
3. Pour the wet ingredients into the dry ingredients and mix until a dough forms.
4. Knead the dough on a lightly floured surface for about 5-7 minutes until it becomes smooth and elastic.
5. Place the dough in a greased bowl, cover it with a clean kitchen towel, and let it rise in a warm place for about 1-2 hours until it doubles in size.
6. Once the dough has risen, punch it down and divide it into equal-sized portions.
7. Flatten each portion of dough into a small circle.
8. Place a spoonful of cooked and chopped sausage pieces (and shredded cheese, if using) in the center of each dough circle.
9. Carefully gather the edges of the dough up and around the filling, pinching them together to seal and form a bread roll.

10. Place the stuffed bread rolls on a baking sheet lined with parchment paper, leaving some space between each roll.
11. Cover the rolls loosely with a clean kitchen towel and let them rise for another 30-45 minutes.
12. Preheat your oven to 350°F (175°C).
13. Once the rolls have risen, bake them in the preheated oven for 15-20 minutes until they are golden brown and cooked through.
14. Remove the Sausage Bread rolls from the oven and let them cool slightly before serving.
15. Enjoy your homemade Sausage Bread rolls warm as a delicious and satisfying snack or meal accompaniment!

Feel free to customize this recipe by using different types of sausages or adding herbs and spices to the filling for extra flavor. You can also brush the tops of the rolls with melted butter and sprinkle with sesame seeds or grated cheese before baking for added texture and flavor.

Apple Cinnamon Bread (사과 시나몬빵)**:** Bread infused with apple chunks and cinnamon for a fragrant and sweet flavor.

Ingredients:

- 2 cups all-purpose flour
- 1/2 cup granulated sugar
- 1 tablespoon baking powder
- 1/2 teaspoon salt
- 1 teaspoon ground cinnamon
- 1/2 cup unsalted butter, melted
- 1 cup milk
- 2 large eggs
- 1 teaspoon vanilla extract
- 1 apple, peeled, cored, and chopped into small pieces

For the Cinnamon Sugar Topping:

- 1/4 cup granulated sugar
- 1 teaspoon ground cinnamon

Instructions:

1. Preheat your oven to 350°F (175°C). Grease a loaf pan or line it with parchment paper.
2. In a large mixing bowl, whisk together the flour, sugar, baking powder, salt, and ground cinnamon.
3. In a separate bowl, mix together the melted butter, milk, eggs, and vanilla extract until well combined.
4. Pour the wet ingredients into the dry ingredients and stir until just combined. Be careful not to overmix.
5. Gently fold in the chopped apple pieces until evenly distributed throughout the batter.
6. Pour the batter into the prepared loaf pan and spread it out evenly.
7. In a small bowl, mix together the granulated sugar and ground cinnamon for the cinnamon sugar topping.

8. Sprinkle the cinnamon sugar mixture evenly over the top of the batter in the loaf pan.
9. Bake in the preheated oven for 45-50 minutes, or until a toothpick inserted into the center comes out clean.
10. Remove the bread from the oven and allow it to cool in the pan for 10-15 minutes before transferring it to a wire rack to cool completely.
11. Once cooled, slice and serve the Apple Cinnamon Bread. Enjoy it warm or at room temperature with a cup of tea or coffee.
12. Store any leftovers in an airtight container at room temperature for up to 3 days, or freeze for longer storage.

Feel free to add chopped nuts or raisins to the batter for added texture and flavor. You can also drizzle a simple glaze made from powdered sugar and milk over the cooled bread for extra sweetness, if desired.

Green Onion Bread (파빵): Bread rolls filled with chopped green onions, adding a savory twist to the bread.

Ingredients:

For the Bread Dough:

- 3 cups all-purpose flour
- 1 tablespoon granulated sugar
- 1 teaspoon salt
- 2 teaspoons instant yeast
- 1 cup warm milk
- 1/4 cup unsalted butter, melted
- 1 large egg

For the Filling:

- 1 cup chopped green onions (scallions)

Instructions:

1. In a large mixing bowl, combine the flour, sugar, salt, and instant yeast.
2. In a separate bowl, whisk together the warm milk, melted butter, and egg.
3. Pour the wet ingredients into the dry ingredients and mix until a dough forms.
4. Knead the dough on a lightly floured surface for about 5-7 minutes until it becomes smooth and elastic.
5. Place the dough in a greased bowl, cover it with a clean kitchen towel, and let it rise in a warm place for about 1-2 hours until it doubles in size.
6. Once the dough has risen, punch it down and divide it into equal-sized portions.
7. Flatten each portion of dough into a small circle.
8. Sprinkle a generous amount of chopped green onions onto the center of each dough circle.
9. Carefully gather the edges of the dough up and around the filling, pinching them together to seal and form a bread roll.

10. Place the stuffed bread rolls on a baking sheet lined with parchment paper, leaving some space between each roll.
11. Cover the rolls loosely with a clean kitchen towel and let them rise for another 30-45 minutes.
12. Preheat your oven to 350°F (175°C).
13. Once the rolls have risen, bake them in the preheated oven for 15-20 minutes until they are golden brown and cooked through.
14. Remove the Green Onion Bread rolls from the oven and let them cool slightly before serving.
15. Enjoy your homemade Green Onion Bread rolls warm as a delicious and savory snack or meal accompaniment!

Feel free to add shredded cheese or cooked bacon bits to the filling for extra flavor. You can also brush the tops of the rolls with melted butter and sprinkle with sesame seeds or grated cheese before baking for added texture and flavor.

Sweet Red Bean Bun (찐빵): Steamed buns filled with sweet red bean paste, a classic Korean dessert.

Ingredients:

For the Dough:

- 2 cups all-purpose flour
- 1 tablespoon granulated sugar
- 1 teaspoon instant yeast
- 1/2 teaspoon salt
- 3/4 cup warm water
- 1 tablespoon vegetable oil

For the Filling:

- 1 cup sweetened red bean paste (store-bought or homemade)

Instructions:

1. In a large mixing bowl, combine the flour, sugar, instant yeast, and salt.
2. Gradually add the warm water and vegetable oil to the dry ingredients, stirring until a dough forms.
3. Knead the dough on a lightly floured surface for about 5-7 minutes until it becomes smooth and elastic.
4. Divide the dough into equal-sized portions, depending on how large you want your buns to be.
5. Flatten each portion of dough into a small circle with your hands.
6. Place a spoonful of sweetened red bean paste in the center of each dough circle.
7. Carefully gather the edges of the dough up and around the filling, pinching them together to seal and form a bun.
8. Place each bun on a small piece of parchment paper to prevent sticking.
9. Arrange the buns in a steamer basket, leaving some space between each bun to allow for expansion.

10. Cover the steamer basket with a clean kitchen towel and let the buns rise for about 20-30 minutes.
11. Meanwhile, bring water to a boil in the steamer pot.
12. Once the buns have risen, place the steamer basket over the boiling water, cover, and steam the buns for 15-20 minutes until they are cooked through and slightly puffed.
13. Remove the steamed buns from the steamer and let them cool slightly before serving.
14. Enjoy your homemade Sweet Red Bean Buns warm as a delicious and comforting treat!

You can also add a sprinkle of sesame seeds on top of each bun before steaming for added flavor and texture. Additionally, feel free to experiment with different fillings such as custard or sweet potato for variation.

Corn Bread (옥수수빵): Bread made with cornmeal and sweet corn kernels, offering a slightly sweet and crunchy texture.

Ingredients:

- 1 cup cornmeal
- 1 cup all-purpose flour
- 1/4 cup granulated sugar
- 1 tablespoon baking powder
- 1/2 teaspoon salt
- 1 cup canned sweet corn kernels, drained
- 1 cup milk
- 1/4 cup unsalted butter, melted
- 2 large eggs

Instructions:

1. Preheat your oven to 375°F (190°C). Grease a 9x9-inch baking pan or line it with parchment paper.
2. In a large mixing bowl, combine the cornmeal, flour, sugar, baking powder, and salt.
3. In a separate bowl, whisk together the milk, melted butter, and eggs until well combined.
4. Pour the wet ingredients into the dry ingredients and mix until just combined. Do not overmix.
5. Gently fold in the sweet corn kernels until evenly distributed throughout the batter.
6. Pour the batter into the prepared baking pan and spread it out evenly.
7. Bake in the preheated oven for 25-30 minutes, or until a toothpick inserted into the center comes out clean.
8. Remove the Corn Bread from the oven and let it cool in the pan for a few minutes before transferring it to a wire rack to cool completely.
9. Once cooled, slice and serve the Corn Bread. Enjoy it warm as a side dish or snack.

Feel free to customize this Corn Bread recipe by adding shredded cheese, chopped jalapenos, or diced bell peppers for extra flavor. You can also drizzle honey or maple syrup on top of the bread for added sweetness.

Cinnamon Raisin Bread (시나몬 레이즌빵)**:** Bread flavored with cinnamon and studded with plump raisins for a sweet and aromatic treat.

Ingredients:

For the Bread Dough:

- 3 cups all-purpose flour
- 1/4 cup granulated sugar
- 1 teaspoon salt
- 2 teaspoons instant yeast
- 1 cup warm milk
- 1/4 cup unsalted butter, melted
- 1 large egg
- 1 cup raisins

For the Cinnamon Sugar Filling:

- 1/4 cup unsalted butter, softened
- 1/4 cup granulated sugar
- 1 tablespoon ground cinnamon

Instructions:

1. In a large mixing bowl, combine the flour, sugar, salt, and instant yeast.
2. In a separate bowl, whisk together the warm milk, melted butter, and egg.
3. Pour the wet ingredients into the dry ingredients and mix until a dough forms.
4. Knead the dough on a lightly floured surface for about 5-7 minutes until it becomes smooth and elastic.
5. Place the dough in a greased bowl, cover it with a clean kitchen towel, and let it rise in a warm place for about 1-2 hours until it doubles in size.
6. Once the dough has risen, punch it down and roll it out into a large rectangle on a lightly floured surface.
7. In a small bowl, mix together the softened butter, sugar, and ground cinnamon to make the cinnamon sugar filling.

8. Spread the cinnamon sugar filling evenly over the surface of the dough rectangle.
9. Sprinkle the raisins evenly over the cinnamon sugar filling.
10. Starting from one of the long sides, roll the dough up tightly into a log.
11. Pinch the seams together to seal and place the rolled dough seam-side down in a greased loaf pan.
12. Cover the loaf pan loosely with a clean kitchen towel and let the dough rise for another 30-45 minutes.
13. Preheat your oven to 350°F (175°C).
14. Once the dough has risen, bake the Cinnamon Raisin Bread in the preheated oven for 30-35 minutes until it is golden brown and sounds hollow when tapped on the bottom.
15. Remove the bread from the oven and let it cool in the pan for a few minutes before transferring it to a wire rack to cool completely.
16. Once cooled, slice and serve the Cinnamon Raisin Bread. Enjoy it warm or toasted with butter or your favorite spread.

Feel free to add chopped nuts or dried fruit such as chopped apricots or cranberries for extra flavor and texture. You can also brush the top of the loaf with a simple glaze made from powdered sugar and milk for added sweetness, if desired.

Kimchi Bread (김치빵)**:** Savory bread rolls filled with spicy and tangy kimchi, perfect for a unique flavor twist.

Ingredients:

For the Bread Dough:

- 3 cups all-purpose flour
- 1 tablespoon granulated sugar
- 1 teaspoon salt
- 2 teaspoons instant yeast
- 1 cup warm milk
- 1/4 cup unsalted butter, melted
- 1 large egg

For the Kimchi Filling:

- 1 cup chopped kimchi, drained
- 1 tablespoon sesame oil
- 1 tablespoon soy sauce
- 1 tablespoon sugar
- 1 tablespoon toasted sesame seeds
- 2 green onions, finely chopped

Instructions:

1. In a large mixing bowl, combine the flour, sugar, salt, and instant yeast.
2. In a separate bowl, whisk together the warm milk, melted butter, and egg.
3. Pour the wet ingredients into the dry ingredients and mix until a dough forms.
4. Knead the dough on a lightly floured surface for about 5-7 minutes until it becomes smooth and elastic.
5. Place the dough in a greased bowl, cover it with a clean kitchen towel, and let it rise in a warm place for about 1-2 hours until it doubles in size.

6. Meanwhile, prepare the kimchi filling. In a mixing bowl, combine the chopped kimchi, sesame oil, soy sauce, sugar, toasted sesame seeds, and chopped green onions. Mix well to combine.
7. Once the dough has risen, punch it down and divide it into equal-sized portions.
8. Flatten each portion of dough into a small circle.
9. Spoon a generous amount of the kimchi filling into the center of each dough circle.
10. Carefully gather the edges of the dough up and around the filling, pinching them together to seal and form a bread roll.
11. Place the stuffed bread rolls on a baking sheet lined with parchment paper, leaving some space between each roll.
12. Cover the rolls loosely with a clean kitchen towel and let them rise for another 30-45 minutes.
13. Preheat your oven to 350°F (175°C).
14. Once the rolls have risen, bake them in the preheated oven for 20-25 minutes until they are golden brown and cooked through.
15. Remove the Kimchi Bread rolls from the oven and let them cool slightly before serving.
16. Enjoy your homemade Kimchi Bread rolls warm as a delicious and flavorful snack or meal accompaniment!

Feel free to adjust the amount of kimchi and seasonings in the filling to suit your taste preferences. You can also add shredded cheese or cooked bacon bits to the filling for extra flavor.

Seaweed Bread (김빵): Bread rolls filled with dried seaweed flakes, adding a salty and umami-rich taste.

Ingredients:

For the Bread Dough:

- 3 cups all-purpose flour
- 1 tablespoon granulated sugar
- 1 teaspoon salt
- 2 teaspoons instant yeast
- 1 cup warm milk
- 1/4 cup unsalted butter, melted
- 1 large egg

For the Seaweed Filling:

- 1 cup dried seaweed flakes (nori), crumbled
- 2 tablespoons sesame oil
- 1 tablespoon soy sauce
- 1 tablespoon sugar
- 1 tablespoon toasted sesame seeds

Instructions:

1. In a large mixing bowl, combine the flour, sugar, salt, and instant yeast.
2. In a separate bowl, whisk together the warm milk, melted butter, and egg.
3. Pour the wet ingredients into the dry ingredients and mix until a dough forms.
4. Knead the dough on a lightly floured surface for about 5-7 minutes until it becomes smooth and elastic.
5. Place the dough in a greased bowl, cover it with a clean kitchen towel, and let it rise in a warm place for about 1-2 hours until it doubles in size.
6. Meanwhile, prepare the seaweed filling. In a mixing bowl, combine the dried seaweed flakes, sesame oil, soy sauce, sugar, and toasted sesame seeds. Mix well to combine.

7. Once the dough has risen, punch it down and divide it into equal-sized portions.
8. Flatten each portion of dough into a small circle.
9. Spoon a generous amount of the seaweed filling into the center of each dough circle.
10. Carefully gather the edges of the dough up and around the filling, pinching them together to seal and form a bread roll.
11. Place the stuffed bread rolls on a baking sheet lined with parchment paper, leaving some space between each roll.
12. Cover the rolls loosely with a clean kitchen towel and let them rise for another 30-45 minutes.
13. Preheat your oven to 350°F (175°C).
14. Once the rolls have risen, bake them in the preheated oven for 20-25 minutes until they are golden brown and cooked through.
15. Remove the Seaweed Bread rolls from the oven and let them cool slightly before serving.
16. Enjoy your homemade Seaweed Bread rolls warm as a delicious and flavorful snack or meal accompaniment!

Feel free to adjust the amount of seaweed and seasonings in the filling to suit your taste preferences. You can also add a sprinkle of shredded cheese on top of each roll before baking for extra flavor.

Chocolate Croissant (초콜릿 크로아상): Buttery croissants filled with rich chocolate, perfect for a decadent breakfast or snack.

Ingredients:

- 1 sheet of puff pastry (store-bought or homemade)
- 4 ounces (115g) dark chocolate, chopped into small pieces
- 1 egg, beaten (for egg wash)
- Powdered sugar (optional, for dusting)

Instructions:

1. Preheat your oven to 400°F (200°C). Line a baking sheet with parchment paper.
2. Roll out the puff pastry sheet on a lightly floured surface into a large rectangle.
3. Using a sharp knife or pizza cutter, cut the rectangle into smaller triangles. You can make them as large or small as you like, depending on your preference.
4. Place a few pieces of chopped dark chocolate at the base of each triangle.
5. Starting from the base, roll up each triangle towards the pointed end, enclosing the chocolate filling inside the pastry.
6. Place the rolled-up croissants on the prepared baking sheet, seam side down.
7. Brush the tops of the croissants with the beaten egg to give them a golden finish.
8. Bake in the preheated oven for 15-20 minutes, or until the croissants are puffed up and golden brown.
9. Remove the Chocolate Croissants from the oven and let them cool slightly on a wire rack.
10. If desired, dust the croissants with powdered sugar before serving.
11. Enjoy your homemade Chocolate Croissants warm or at room temperature as a decadent breakfast treat or snack.

Feel free to experiment with different types of chocolate, such as milk chocolate or white chocolate, for the filling. You can also add chopped nuts or a sprinkle of sea salt for extra flavor and texture.

Custard Cream Bun (크림빵): Soft bread rolls filled with creamy custard filling, a beloved Korean bakery staple.

Ingredients:

For the Bread Dough:

- 3 cups all-purpose flour
- 1/4 cup granulated sugar
- 1 teaspoon salt
- 2 teaspoons instant yeast
- 1 cup warm milk
- 1/4 cup unsalted butter, melted
- 1 large egg

For the Custard Filling:

- 2 cups milk
- 1/2 cup granulated sugar
- 1/4 cup cornstarch
- 4 large egg yolks
- 1 teaspoon vanilla extract

Instructions:

1. In a large mixing bowl, combine the flour, sugar, salt, and instant yeast.
2. In a separate bowl, whisk together the warm milk, melted butter, and egg.
3. Pour the wet ingredients into the dry ingredients and mix until a dough forms.
4. Knead the dough on a lightly floured surface for about 5-7 minutes until it becomes smooth and elastic.
5. Place the dough in a greased bowl, cover it with a clean kitchen towel, and let it rise in a warm place for about 1-2 hours until it doubles in size.
6. Meanwhile, prepare the custard filling. In a saucepan, heat the milk over medium heat until it is steaming but not boiling.

7. In a mixing bowl, whisk together the sugar, cornstarch, and egg yolks until smooth and creamy.
8. Gradually pour the hot milk into the egg mixture, whisking constantly to prevent the eggs from scrambling.
9. Return the mixture to the saucepan and cook over medium heat, stirring constantly, until the custard thickens and coats the back of a spoon.
10. Remove the custard from the heat and stir in the vanilla extract. Transfer the custard to a bowl and cover it with plastic wrap, pressing the wrap directly onto the surface of the custard to prevent a skin from forming. Refrigerate until completely chilled.
11. Once the dough has risen, punch it down and divide it into equal-sized portions.
12. Flatten each portion of dough into a small circle.
13. Spoon a generous amount of chilled custard filling into the center of each dough circle.
14. Carefully gather the edges of the dough up and around the filling, pinching them together to seal and form a bread roll.
15. Place the stuffed bread rolls on a baking sheet lined with parchment paper, leaving some space between each roll.
16. Cover the rolls loosely with a clean kitchen towel and let them rise for another 30-45 minutes.
17. Preheat your oven to 350°F (175°C).
18. Once the rolls have risen, bake them in the preheated oven for 20-25 minutes until they are golden brown and cooked through.
19. Remove the Custard Cream Buns from the oven and let them cool slightly before serving.
20. Enjoy your homemade Custard Cream Buns warm as a delicious and creamy treat!

Feel free to dust the tops of the buns with powdered sugar for added sweetness before serving, if desired. You can also add a sprinkle of cinnamon or cocoa powder to the custard filling for extra flavor.

Rice Cake Bread (떡빵): Bread rolls stuffed with sweet and chewy rice cakes, offering a delightful combination of textures.

Ingredients:

For the Bread Dough:

- 3 cups all-purpose flour
- 1/4 cup granulated sugar
- 1 teaspoon salt
- 2 teaspoons instant yeast
- 1 cup warm milk
- 1/4 cup unsalted butter, melted
- 1 large egg

For the Rice Cake Filling:

- 1 cup sweet rice flour (glutinous rice flour)
- 1/4 cup granulated sugar
- 3/4 cup water
- 1/2 cup sweet red bean paste (optional)
- Sesame seeds for garnish (optional)

Instructions:

1. In a large mixing bowl, combine the flour, sugar, salt, and instant yeast.
2. In a separate bowl, whisk together the warm milk, melted butter, and egg.
3. Pour the wet ingredients into the dry ingredients and mix until a dough forms.
4. Knead the dough on a lightly floured surface for about 5-7 minutes until it becomes smooth and elastic.
5. Place the dough in a greased bowl, cover it with a clean kitchen towel, and let it rise in a warm place for about 1-2 hours until it doubles in size.
6. Meanwhile, prepare the rice cake filling. In a microwave-safe bowl, combine the sweet rice flour, sugar, and water. Mix well to combine.

7. Microwave the mixture on high for 1 minute. Stir well and microwave for another 1-2 minutes until the mixture becomes thick and sticky, resembling a dough.
8. Let the rice cake dough cool slightly, then divide it into small portions, rolling each portion into a small ball.
9. Once the dough has risen, punch it down and divide it into equal-sized portions.
10. Flatten each portion of dough into a small circle.
11. Place a small portion of sweet red bean paste (if using) and a rice cake ball in the center of each dough circle.
12. Carefully gather the edges of the dough up and around the filling, pinching them together to seal and form a bread roll.
13. Place the stuffed bread rolls on a baking sheet lined with parchment paper, leaving some space between each roll.
14. Cover the rolls loosely with a clean kitchen towel and let them rise for another 30-45 minutes.
15. Preheat your oven to 350°F (175°C).
16. Once the rolls have risen, sprinkle sesame seeds on top of each roll for garnish, if desired.
17. Bake the Rice Cake Bread rolls in the preheated oven for 20-25 minutes until they are golden brown and cooked through.
18. Remove the rolls from the oven and let them cool slightly before serving.
19. Enjoy your homemade Rice Cake Bread warm as a delightful and comforting treat!

Feel free to adjust the amount of sweet red bean paste or omit it entirely based on your preference. You can also experiment with different fillings such as nutella or fruit preserves for variation.

Sweet Potato Cream Bread (고구마 크림빵): Bread filled with a creamy sweet potato filling, offering a comforting and indulgent treat.

Ingredients:

For the Bread Dough:

- 3 cups all-purpose flour
- 1/4 cup granulated sugar
- 1 teaspoon salt
- 2 teaspoons instant yeast
- 1 cup warm milk
- 1/4 cup unsalted butter, melted
- 1 large egg

For the Sweet Potato Filling:

- 1 large sweet potato, peeled and diced
- 1/4 cup granulated sugar
- 1/4 cup milk
- 2 tablespoons unsalted butter
- 1/2 teaspoon vanilla extract
- Pinch of salt

Instructions:

1. In a large mixing bowl, combine the flour, sugar, salt, and instant yeast.
2. In a separate bowl, whisk together the warm milk, melted butter, and egg.
3. Pour the wet ingredients into the dry ingredients and mix until a dough forms.
4. Knead the dough on a lightly floured surface for about 5-7 minutes until it becomes smooth and elastic.
5. Place the dough in a greased bowl, cover it with a clean kitchen towel, and let it rise in a warm place for about 1-2 hours until it doubles in size.
6. Meanwhile, prepare the sweet potato filling. Place the diced sweet potato in a saucepan and cover with water. Bring to a boil and cook until the sweet potato is

fork-tender, about 10-15 minutes. Drain the sweet potato and transfer it to a mixing bowl.
7. Mash the cooked sweet potato with a fork or potato masher until smooth.
8. In a small saucepan, combine the mashed sweet potato, sugar, milk, butter, vanilla extract, and salt. Cook over medium heat, stirring constantly, until the mixture is thick and creamy, about 5-7 minutes. Remove from heat and let it cool slightly.
9. Once the dough has risen, punch it down and divide it into equal-sized portions.
10. Flatten each portion of dough into a small circle.
11. Spoon a generous amount of sweet potato filling into the center of each dough circle.
12. Carefully gather the edges of the dough up and around the filling, pinching them together to seal and form a bread roll.
13. Place the stuffed bread rolls on a baking sheet lined with parchment paper, leaving some space between each roll.
14. Cover the rolls loosely with a clean kitchen towel and let them rise for another 30-45 minutes.
15. Preheat your oven to 350°F (175°C).
16. Once the rolls have risen, bake them in the preheated oven for 20-25 minutes until they are golden brown and cooked through.
17. Remove the Sweet Potato Cream Bread rolls from the oven and let them cool slightly before serving.
18. Enjoy your homemade Sweet Potato Cream Bread warm as a comforting and indulgent treat!

Feel free to dust the tops of the rolls with powdered sugar for added sweetness before serving, if desired. You can also add a sprinkle of cinnamon or nutmeg to the sweet potato filling for extra flavor.

Honey Butter Bread (꿀버터빵): Soft bread rolls coated in a sweet and buttery honey glaze, perfect for a sweet and indulgent snack.

Ingredients:

For the Bread Dough:

- 3 cups all-purpose flour
- 1/4 cup granulated sugar
- 1 teaspoon salt
- 2 teaspoons instant yeast
- 1 cup warm milk
- 1/4 cup unsalted butter, melted
- 1 large egg

For the Honey Butter Glaze:

- 1/4 cup unsalted butter
- 1/4 cup honey
- Pinch of salt

Instructions:

1. In a large mixing bowl, combine the flour, sugar, salt, and instant yeast.
2. In a separate bowl, whisk together the warm milk, melted butter, and egg.
3. Pour the wet ingredients into the dry ingredients and mix until a dough forms.
4. Knead the dough on a lightly floured surface for about 5-7 minutes until it becomes smooth and elastic.
5. Place the dough in a greased bowl, cover it with a clean kitchen towel, and let it rise in a warm place for about 1-2 hours until it doubles in size.
6. Once the dough has risen, punch it down and divide it into equal-sized portions.
7. Roll each portion of dough into a ball and place them on a baking sheet lined with parchment paper, leaving some space between each roll.
8. Cover the rolls loosely with a clean kitchen towel and let them rise for another 30-45 minutes.

9. Preheat your oven to 350°F (175°C).
10. Bake the rolls in the preheated oven for 15-20 minutes until they are golden brown and cooked through.
11. While the rolls are baking, prepare the honey butter glaze. In a small saucepan, melt the butter over medium heat. Stir in the honey and a pinch of salt, and cook for 1-2 minutes until the mixture is smooth and well combined. Remove from heat.
12. Once the rolls are done baking, remove them from the oven and immediately brush the tops with the honey butter glaze while they are still warm.
13. Let the Honey Butter Bread rolls cool slightly before serving.
14. Enjoy your homemade Honey Butter Bread warm as a sweet and indulgent snack!

Feel free to sprinkle some sesame seeds or chopped nuts on top of the rolls before baking for added flavor and texture. You can also drizzle extra honey butter glaze over the rolls before serving for an extra decadent touch.

Cheese Bread (치즈빵): Soft bread rolls filled with gooey melted cheese, offering a savory and satisfying flavor.

Ingredients:

For the Bread Dough:

- 3 cups all-purpose flour
- 1/4 cup granulated sugar
- 1 teaspoon salt
- 2 teaspoons instant yeast
- 1 cup warm milk
- 1/4 cup unsalted butter, melted
- 1 large egg

For the Cheese Filling:

- 1 cup shredded cheese (cheddar, mozzarella, or your favorite cheese)
- Optional: 1/4 cup cream cheese (for extra creaminess)

Instructions:

1. In a large mixing bowl, combine the flour, sugar, salt, and instant yeast.
2. In a separate bowl, whisk together the warm milk, melted butter, and egg.
3. Pour the wet ingredients into the dry ingredients and mix until a dough forms.
4. Knead the dough on a lightly floured surface for about 5-7 minutes until it becomes smooth and elastic.
5. Place the dough in a greased bowl, cover it with a clean kitchen towel, and let it rise in a warm place for about 1-2 hours until it doubles in size.
6. Once the dough has risen, punch it down and divide it into equal-sized portions.
7. Flatten each portion of dough into a small circle.
8. Place a generous amount of shredded cheese (and cream cheese, if using) in the center of each dough circle.
9. Carefully gather the edges of the dough up and around the filling, pinching them together to seal and form a bread roll.

10. Place the stuffed bread rolls on a baking sheet lined with parchment paper, leaving some space between each roll.
11. Cover the rolls loosely with a clean kitchen towel and let them rise for another 30-45 minutes.
12. Preheat your oven to 350°F (175°C).
13. Once the rolls have risen, bake them in the preheated oven for 20-25 minutes until they are golden brown and cooked through.
14. Remove the Cheese Bread rolls from the oven and let them cool slightly before serving.
15. Enjoy your homemade Cheese Bread warm as a savory and delicious snack or accompaniment to your favorite meal!

Feel free to customize the cheese filling by adding herbs, spices, or cooked bacon for extra flavor. You can also brush the tops of the rolls with melted butter and sprinkle with garlic powder or grated Parmesan cheese before baking for added flavor.

Almond Cream Bread (아몬드 크림빵): Bread rolls filled with creamy almond paste, topped with sliced almonds for a crunchy texture.

Ingredients:

For the Bread Dough:

- 3 cups all-purpose flour
- 1/4 cup granulated sugar
- 1 teaspoon salt
- 2 teaspoons instant yeast
- 1 cup warm milk
- 1/4 cup unsalted butter, melted
- 1 large egg

For the Almond Cream Filling:

- 1 cup almond flour
- 1/4 cup granulated sugar
- 1/4 cup unsalted butter, softened
- 1 large egg
- 1 teaspoon almond extract

For Topping:

- Sliced almonds

Instructions:

1. In a large mixing bowl, combine the flour, sugar, salt, and instant yeast.
2. In a separate bowl, whisk together the warm milk, melted butter, and egg.
3. Pour the wet ingredients into the dry ingredients and mix until a dough forms.
4. Knead the dough on a lightly floured surface for about 5-7 minutes until it becomes smooth and elastic.

5. Place the dough in a greased bowl, cover it with a clean kitchen towel, and let it rise in a warm place for about 1-2 hours until it doubles in size.
6. Meanwhile, prepare the almond cream filling. In a mixing bowl, combine the almond flour, sugar, softened butter, egg, and almond extract. Mix until smooth and creamy.
7. Once the dough has risen, punch it down and divide it into equal-sized portions.
8. Flatten each portion of dough into a small circle.
9. Spoon a generous amount of almond cream filling into the center of each dough circle.
10. Carefully gather the edges of the dough up and around the filling, pinching them together to seal and form a bread roll.
11. Place the stuffed bread rolls on a baking sheet lined with parchment paper, leaving some space between each roll.
12. Cover the rolls loosely with a clean kitchen towel and let them rise for another 30-45 minutes.
13. Preheat your oven to 350°F (175°C).
14. Once the rolls have risen, sprinkle sliced almonds on top of each roll for topping.
15. Bake the Almond Cream Bread rolls in the preheated oven for 20-25 minutes until they are golden brown and cooked through.
16. Remove the rolls from the oven and let them cool slightly before serving.
17. Enjoy your homemade Almond Cream Bread warm as a delicious and nutty treat!

Feel free to dust the tops of the rolls with powdered sugar for added sweetness before serving, if desired. You can also add a sprinkle of cinnamon or drizzle of honey on top for extra flavor.

Caramel Bread (카라멜빵): Bread rolls drizzled with rich caramel sauce, offering a sweet and indulgent flavor.

Ingredients:

For the Bread Dough:

- 3 cups all-purpose flour
- 1/4 cup granulated sugar
- 1 teaspoon salt
- 2 teaspoons instant yeast
- 1 cup warm milk
- 1/4 cup unsalted butter, melted
- 1 large egg

For the Caramel Sauce:

- 1/2 cup granulated sugar
- 1/4 cup unsalted butter
- 1/4 cup heavy cream
- 1 teaspoon vanilla extract
- Pinch of salt

Instructions:

1. In a large mixing bowl, combine the flour, sugar, salt, and instant yeast.
2. In a separate bowl, whisk together the warm milk, melted butter, and egg.
3. Pour the wet ingredients into the dry ingredients and mix until a dough forms.
4. Knead the dough on a lightly floured surface for about 5-7 minutes until it becomes smooth and elastic.
5. Place the dough in a greased bowl, cover it with a clean kitchen towel, and let it rise in a warm place for about 1-2 hours until it doubles in size.
6. Meanwhile, prepare the caramel sauce. In a saucepan, heat the sugar over medium heat, stirring constantly with a wooden spoon until it melts and turns golden brown.

7. Add the butter to the melted sugar and stir until melted and well combined.
8. Slowly pour in the heavy cream while stirring continuously until the sauce is smooth and creamy.
9. Remove the caramel sauce from the heat and stir in the vanilla extract and a pinch of salt. Set aside to cool slightly.
10. Once the dough has risen, punch it down and divide it into equal-sized portions.
11. Flatten each portion of dough into a small circle.
12. Place the flattened dough circles on a baking sheet lined with parchment paper, leaving some space between each roll.
13. Cover the rolls loosely with a clean kitchen towel and let them rise for another 30-45 minutes.
14. Preheat your oven to 350°F (175°C).
15. Once the rolls have risen, bake them in the preheated oven for 20-25 minutes until they are golden brown and cooked through.
16. Remove the rolls from the oven and let them cool slightly.
17. Drizzle the warm caramel sauce over the Caramel Bread rolls.
18. Enjoy your homemade Caramel Bread warm as a sweet and indulgent treat!

Feel free to sprinkle some chopped nuts or sea salt on top of the caramel sauce for added flavor and texture. You can also add a sprinkle of cinnamon or nutmeg to the dough for extra flavor.

Black Sesame Bread (검은깨빵): Bread rolls infused with ground black sesame seeds for a nutty flavor and striking color.

Ingredients:

For the Bread Dough:

- 3 cups all-purpose flour
- 1/4 cup granulated sugar
- 1 teaspoon salt
- 2 teaspoons instant yeast
- 1 cup warm milk
- 1/4 cup unsalted butter, melted
- 1 large egg
- 1/4 cup ground black sesame seeds

For Topping (optional):

- Whole black sesame seeds

Instructions:

1. In a blender or food processor, grind the black sesame seeds until they form a fine powder. Set aside.
2. In a large mixing bowl, combine the flour, sugar, salt, and instant yeast.
3. In a separate bowl, whisk together the warm milk, melted butter, egg, and ground black sesame seeds.
4. Pour the wet ingredients into the dry ingredients and mix until a dough forms.
5. Knead the dough on a lightly floured surface for about 5-7 minutes until it becomes smooth and elastic.
6. Place the dough in a greased bowl, cover it with a clean kitchen towel, and let it rise in a warm place for about 1-2 hours until it doubles in size.
7. Once the dough has risen, punch it down and divide it into equal-sized portions.
8. Flatten each portion of dough into a small circle.

9. Roll up each circle of dough into a tight roll, tucking in the edges to form a bread roll shape.
10. Place the rolls on a baking sheet lined with parchment paper, leaving some space between each roll.
11. Cover the rolls loosely with a clean kitchen towel and let them rise for another 30-45 minutes.
12. Preheat your oven to 350°F (175°C).
13. Once the rolls have risen, sprinkle whole black sesame seeds on top of each roll for topping, if desired.
14. Bake the Black Sesame Bread rolls in the preheated oven for 20-25 minutes until they are golden brown and cooked through.
15. Remove the rolls from the oven and let them cool slightly before serving.
16. Enjoy your homemade Black Sesame Bread warm as a delicious and nutty treat!

Feel free to experiment with the amount of ground black sesame seeds to adjust the intensity of the flavor. You can also add a teaspoon of honey or maple syrup to the dough for a touch of sweetness, if desired.

Sweet Red Bean Roll (팥 롤빵): Soft bread rolls filled with sweet red bean paste and rolled into a log shape.

Ingredients:

For the Bread Dough:

- 3 cups all-purpose flour
- 1/4 cup granulated sugar
- 1 teaspoon salt
- 2 teaspoons instant yeast
- 1 cup warm milk
- 1/4 cup unsalted butter, melted
- 1 large egg

For the Sweet Red Bean Filling:

- 1 cup sweet red bean paste (store-bought or homemade)
- Optional: 1 tablespoon honey or maple syrup (for extra sweetness)

Instructions:

1. In a large mixing bowl, combine the flour, sugar, salt, and instant yeast.
2. In a separate bowl, whisk together the warm milk, melted butter, and egg.
3. Pour the wet ingredients into the dry ingredients and mix until a dough forms.
4. Knead the dough on a lightly floured surface for about 5-7 minutes until it becomes smooth and elastic.
5. Place the dough in a greased bowl, cover it with a clean kitchen towel, and let it rise in a warm place for about 1-2 hours until it doubles in size.
6. Once the dough has risen, punch it down and divide it into equal-sized portions.
7. Roll out each portion of dough into a rectangular shape, about 1/4 inch thick.
8. Spread a layer of sweet red bean paste evenly over the surface of each dough rectangle, leaving a small border around the edges.
9. Optional: Drizzle a little honey or maple syrup over the red bean paste for extra sweetness.

10. Starting from one long side, tightly roll up each dough rectangle into a log shape.
11. Place the rolled-up dough logs seam-side down on a baking sheet lined with parchment paper, leaving some space between each roll.
12. Cover the rolls loosely with a clean kitchen towel and let them rise for another 30-45 minutes.
13. Preheat your oven to 350°F (175°C).
14. Once the rolls have risen, bake them in the preheated oven for 20-25 minutes until they are golden brown and cooked through.
15. Remove the rolls from the oven and let them cool slightly before serving.
16. Enjoy your homemade Sweet Red Bean Rolls warm as a delicious and comforting treat!

Feel free to dust the tops of the rolls with powdered sugar for added sweetness before serving, if desired. You can also sprinkle some sesame seeds on top of the rolls for extra flavor and texture.

Cream Corn Bread (크림 옥수수빵): Bread rolls filled with creamy sweet corn filling, offering a sweet and savory flavor profile.

Ingredients:

For the Bread Dough:

- 3 cups all-purpose flour
- 1/4 cup granulated sugar
- 1 teaspoon salt
- 2 teaspoons instant yeast
- 1 cup warm milk
- 1/4 cup unsalted butter, melted
- 1 large egg

For the Cream Corn Filling:

- 1 cup sweet corn kernels (fresh, frozen, or canned)
- 1/4 cup cream cheese, softened
- 2 tablespoons mayonnaise
- 2 tablespoons grated Parmesan cheese
- 1 tablespoon chopped fresh chives (optional)
- Salt and pepper to taste

Instructions:

1. In a large mixing bowl, combine the flour, sugar, salt, and instant yeast.
2. In a separate bowl, whisk together the warm milk, melted butter, and egg.
3. Pour the wet ingredients into the dry ingredients and mix until a dough forms.
4. Knead the dough on a lightly floured surface for about 5-7 minutes until it becomes smooth and elastic.
5. Place the dough in a greased bowl, cover it with a clean kitchen towel, and let it rise in a warm place for about 1-2 hours until it doubles in size.
6. Meanwhile, prepare the cream corn filling. In a mixing bowl, combine the sweet corn kernels, cream cheese, mayonnaise, grated Parmesan cheese, chopped fresh chives (if using), salt, and pepper. Mix until well combined and creamy.
7. Once the dough has risen, punch it down and divide it into equal-sized portions.

8. Flatten each portion of dough into a small circle.
9. Spoon a generous amount of the cream corn filling into the center of each dough circle.
10. Carefully gather the edges of the dough up and around the filling, pinching them together to seal and form a bread roll.
11. Place the stuffed bread rolls on a baking sheet lined with parchment paper, leaving some space between each roll.
12. Cover the rolls loosely with a clean kitchen towel and let them rise for another 30-45 minutes.
13. Preheat your oven to 350°F (175°C).
14. Once the rolls have risen, bake them in the preheated oven for 20-25 minutes until they are golden brown and cooked through.
15. Remove the rolls from the oven and let them cool slightly before serving.
16. Enjoy your homemade Cream Corn Bread warm as a delicious and savory treat!

Feel free to sprinkle some extra grated Parmesan cheese on top of the rolls before baking for added flavor. You can also add a sprinkle of paprika or chili powder to the cream corn filling for a hint of spice.

Sweet Potato Walnut Bread (고구마 호두빵): Bread made with mashed sweet potatoes and studded with chopped walnuts for added texture and flavor.

Ingredients:

For the Bread Dough:

- 2 cups all-purpose flour
- 1/2 cup granulated sugar
- 1 teaspoon salt
- 2 teaspoons instant yeast
- 1/2 cup mashed sweet potatoes (cooked and cooled)
- 1/4 cup unsalted butter, melted
- 1/2 cup warm milk
- 1 large egg
- 1 teaspoon vanilla extract

For the Filling (optional):

- 1/2 cup chopped walnuts

Instructions:

1. In a large mixing bowl, combine the flour, sugar, salt, and instant yeast.
2. In a separate bowl, whisk together the mashed sweet potatoes, melted butter, warm milk, egg, and vanilla extract.
3. Pour the wet ingredients into the dry ingredients and mix until a dough forms.
4. Knead the dough on a lightly floured surface for about 5-7 minutes until it becomes smooth and elastic.
5. Place the dough in a greased bowl, cover it with a clean kitchen towel, and let it rise in a warm place for about 1-2 hours until it doubles in size.
6. Once the dough has risen, punch it down and divide it into equal-sized portions.
7. Flatten each portion of dough into a small rectangle.
8. If using, sprinkle some chopped walnuts evenly over the surface of each dough rectangle.

9. Roll up each dough rectangle into a tight log, tucking in the edges to seal.
10. Place the rolled-up dough logs seam-side down on a baking sheet lined with parchment paper, leaving some space between each roll.
11. Cover the rolls loosely with a clean kitchen towel and let them rise for another 30-45 minutes.
12. Preheat your oven to 350°F (175°C).
13. Once the rolls have risen, bake them in the preheated oven for 20-25 minutes until they are golden brown and cooked through.
14. Remove the rolls from the oven and let them cool slightly before serving.
15. Enjoy your homemade Sweet Potato Walnut Bread warm as a delicious and nutty treat!

Feel free to customize this recipe by adding cinnamon or nutmeg to the dough for extra flavor. You can also brush the tops of the rolls with melted butter and sprinkle with sugar before baking for added sweetness and crunch.

Cinnamon Sugar Breadsticks (시나몬 슈가 브레드스틱): Crispy breadsticks coated in cinnamon sugar, perfect for a sweet and crunchy snack.

Ingredients:

For the Dough:

- 2 cups all-purpose flour
- 1 tablespoon granulated sugar
- 1 teaspoon salt
- 1 tablespoon instant yeast
- 3/4 cup warm water
- 2 tablespoons unsalted butter, melted

For the Cinnamon Sugar Coating:

- 1/4 cup granulated sugar
- 1 tablespoon ground cinnamon
- 1/4 cup unsalted butter, melted

Instructions:

1. In a large mixing bowl, combine the flour, sugar, salt, and instant yeast.
2. Gradually add the warm water and melted butter to the dry ingredients, mixing until a dough forms.
3. Knead the dough on a lightly floured surface for about 5-7 minutes until it becomes smooth and elastic.
4. Place the dough in a greased bowl, cover it with a clean kitchen towel, and let it rise in a warm place for about 1 hour until it doubles in size.
5. Preheat your oven to 375°F (190°C). Line a baking sheet with parchment paper.
6. Punch down the risen dough and divide it into equal-sized portions.
7. Roll each portion of dough into a long rope, about 10-12 inches in length.
8. Place the dough ropes on the prepared baking sheet, leaving some space between each rope.

9. Bake the breadsticks in the preheated oven for 12-15 minutes until they are golden brown and crispy.
10. While the breadsticks are baking, prepare the cinnamon sugar coating. In a shallow bowl, mix together the granulated sugar and ground cinnamon.
11. Once the breadsticks are baked and still warm, brush each breadstick with melted butter, then roll them in the cinnamon sugar mixture until they are well coated.
12. Place the coated breadsticks on a wire rack to cool completely.
13. Enjoy your homemade Cinnamon Sugar Breadsticks as a sweet and crunchy snack!

Feel free to adjust the amount of cinnamon sugar coating according to your preference.

You can also serve these breadsticks with a side of chocolate sauce or cream cheese frosting for dipping, if desired.

Potato Bacon Bread (감자 베이컨빵)**:** Bread rolls filled with mashed potatoes and crispy bacon pieces, offering a savory and satisfying flavor combination.

Ingredients:

For the Bread Dough:

- 3 cups all-purpose flour
- 1/4 cup granulated sugar
- 1 teaspoon salt
- 2 teaspoons instant yeast
- 1 cup warm milk
- 1/4 cup unsalted butter, melted
- 1 large egg

For the Filling:

- 2 large potatoes, peeled and diced
- 6 slices bacon, cooked until crispy and chopped
- 1/4 cup shredded cheddar cheese
- Salt and pepper to taste

Instructions:

1. In a large mixing bowl, combine the flour, sugar, salt, and instant yeast.
2. In a separate bowl, whisk together the warm milk, melted butter, and egg.
3. Pour the wet ingredients into the dry ingredients and mix until a dough forms.
4. Knead the dough on a lightly floured surface for about 5-7 minutes until it becomes smooth and elastic.
5. Place the dough in a greased bowl, cover it with a clean kitchen towel, and let it rise in a warm place for about 1-2 hours until it doubles in size.
6. Meanwhile, prepare the filling. Boil the diced potatoes in salted water until they are fork-tender. Drain the potatoes and mash them until smooth. Season with salt and pepper to taste.
7. Once the dough has risen, punch it down and divide it into equal-sized portions.

8. Flatten each portion of dough into a small circle.
9. Spread a layer of mashed potatoes evenly over the surface of each dough circle.
10. Sprinkle the chopped bacon and shredded cheddar cheese over the mashed potatoes.
11. Carefully roll up each dough circle into a tight log, tucking in the edges to seal and form a bread roll.
12. Place the stuffed bread rolls on a baking sheet lined with parchment paper, leaving some space between each roll.
13. Cover the rolls loosely with a clean kitchen towel and let them rise for another 30-45 minutes.
14. Preheat your oven to 350°F (175°C).
15. Once the rolls have risen, bake them in the preheated oven for 20-25 minutes until they are golden brown and cooked through.
16. Remove the rolls from the oven and let them cool slightly before serving.
17. Enjoy your homemade Potato Bacon Bread warm as a delicious and savory treat!

Feel free to add some chopped green onions or herbs to the mashed potato filling for added flavor. You can also brush the tops of the rolls with melted butter before baking for a golden crust.

Cheese Onion Bread (치즈 양파빵): Bread rolls filled with melted cheese and caramelized onions, offering a rich and savory taste.

Ingredients:

For the Bread Dough:

- 3 cups all-purpose flour
- 1/4 cup granulated sugar
- 1 teaspoon salt
- 2 teaspoons instant yeast
- 1 cup warm milk
- 1/4 cup unsalted butter, melted
- 1 large egg

For the Filling:

- 1 large onion, thinly sliced
- 2 tablespoons unsalted butter
- 1 cup shredded cheese (cheddar, mozzarella, or your favorite cheese)
- Salt and pepper to taste

Instructions:

1. In a large mixing bowl, combine the flour, sugar, salt, and instant yeast.
2. In a separate bowl, whisk together the warm milk, melted butter, and egg.
3. Pour the wet ingredients into the dry ingredients and mix until a dough forms.
4. Knead the dough on a lightly floured surface for about 5-7 minutes until it becomes smooth and elastic.
5. Place the dough in a greased bowl, cover it with a clean kitchen towel, and let it rise in a warm place for about 1-2 hours until it doubles in size.
6. Meanwhile, prepare the filling. In a skillet, melt the butter over medium heat. Add the thinly sliced onions and cook, stirring occasionally, until they are soft and caramelized, about 15-20 minutes. Season with salt and pepper to taste.
7. Once the dough has risen, punch it down and divide it into equal-sized portions.

8. Flatten each portion of dough into a small circle.
9. Spoon a layer of caramelized onions onto the surface of each dough circle, leaving a small border around the edges.
10. Sprinkle the shredded cheese evenly over the caramelized onions.
11. Carefully roll up each dough circle into a tight log, tucking in the edges to seal and form a bread roll.
12. Place the stuffed bread rolls on a baking sheet lined with parchment paper, leaving some space between each roll.
13. Cover the rolls loosely with a clean kitchen towel and let them rise for another 30-45 minutes.
14. Preheat your oven to 350°F (175°C).
15. Once the rolls have risen, bake them in the preheated oven for 20-25 minutes until they are golden brown and cooked through.
16. Remove the rolls from the oven and let them cool slightly before serving.
17. Enjoy your homemade Cheese Onion Bread warm as a delicious and savory treat!

Feel free to add some herbs like thyme or rosemary to the caramelized onions for added flavor. You can also brush the tops of the rolls with melted butter before baking for a golden crust.

Matcha Red Bean Bun (녹차 팥빵): Soft bread rolls infused with matcha green tea powder and filled with sweet red bean paste.

Ingredients:

For the Bread Dough:

- 3 cups all-purpose flour
- 1/4 cup granulated sugar
- 1 teaspoon salt
- 2 teaspoons instant yeast
- 1 cup warm milk
- 1/4 cup unsalted butter, melted
- 2 tablespoons matcha green tea powder

For the Filling:

- 1 cup sweet red bean paste (store-bought or homemade)

Instructions:

1. In a large mixing bowl, combine the flour, sugar, salt, and instant yeast.
2. In a separate bowl, whisk together the warm milk, melted butter, and matcha green tea powder until the matcha powder is fully dissolved.
3. Pour the wet ingredients into the dry ingredients and mix until a dough forms.
4. Knead the dough on a lightly floured surface for about 5-7 minutes until it becomes smooth and elastic.
5. Place the dough in a greased bowl, cover it with a clean kitchen towel, and let it rise in a warm place for about 1-2 hours until it doubles in size.
6. Once the dough has risen, punch it down and divide it into equal-sized portions.
7. Flatten each portion of dough into a small circle.
8. Spoon a dollop of sweet red bean paste onto the center of each dough circle.
9. Carefully gather the edges of the dough up and around the filling, pinching them together to seal and form a bun.

10. Place the filled buns on a baking sheet lined with parchment paper, leaving some space between each bun.
11. Cover the buns loosely with a clean kitchen towel and let them rise for another 30-45 minutes.
12. Preheat your oven to 350°F (175°C).
13. Once the buns have risen, bake them in the preheated oven for 15-20 minutes until they are golden brown and cooked through.
14. Remove the buns from the oven and let them cool slightly before serving.
15. Enjoy your homemade Matcha Red Bean Buns warm as a delicious and flavorful treat!

Feel free to brush the tops of the buns with a beaten egg wash before baking for a shiny finish. You can also sprinkle some sesame seeds or powdered sugar on top of the buns for added flavor and decoration.

Apple Walnut Bread (사과 호두빵): Bread rolls filled with diced apples and chopped walnuts, offering a sweet and nutty flavor.

Ingredients:

For the Bread Dough:

- 3 cups all-purpose flour
- 1/4 cup granulated sugar
- 1 teaspoon salt
- 2 teaspoons instant yeast
- 1 cup warm milk
- 1/4 cup unsalted butter, melted
- 1 large egg

For the Filling:

- 2 medium apples, peeled, cored, and diced
- 1/2 cup chopped walnuts
- 1/4 cup brown sugar
- 1 teaspoon ground cinnamon
- 1 tablespoon lemon juice
- 2 tablespoons unsalted butter

Instructions:

1. In a large mixing bowl, combine the flour, sugar, salt, and instant yeast.
2. In a separate bowl, whisk together the warm milk, melted butter, and egg.
3. Pour the wet ingredients into the dry ingredients and mix until a dough forms.
4. Knead the dough on a lightly floured surface for about 5-7 minutes until it becomes smooth and elastic.
5. Place the dough in a greased bowl, cover it with a clean kitchen towel, and let it rise in a warm place for about 1-2 hours until it doubles in size.
6. Meanwhile, prepare the filling. In a skillet, melt the butter over medium heat. Add the diced apples, chopped walnuts, brown sugar, ground cinnamon, and lemon

juice. Cook, stirring occasionally, until the apples are soft and caramelized, about 8-10 minutes. Remove from heat and let the filling cool slightly.
7. Once the dough has risen, punch it down and divide it into equal-sized portions.
8. Flatten each portion of dough into a small circle.
9. Spoon a generous amount of the apple walnut filling onto the center of each dough circle.
10. Carefully gather the edges of the dough up and around the filling, pinching them together to seal and form a bread roll.
11. Place the stuffed bread rolls on a baking sheet lined with parchment paper, leaving some space between each roll.
12. Cover the rolls loosely with a clean kitchen towel and let them rise for another 30-45 minutes.
13. Preheat your oven to 350°F (175°C).
14. Once the rolls have risen, bake them in the preheated oven for 20-25 minutes until they are golden brown and cooked through.
15. Remove the rolls from the oven and let them cool slightly before serving.
16. Enjoy your homemade Apple Walnut Bread warm as a delicious and flavorful treat!

Feel free to sprinkle some additional brown sugar or cinnamon on top of the rolls before baking for added sweetness and flavor. You can also brush the tops of the rolls with melted butter for a shiny finish.

Pumpkin Bread (호박빵): Bread made with pureed pumpkin for a moist and flavorful texture, perfect for autumn baking.

Ingredients:

- 1 3/4 cups all-purpose flour
- 1 teaspoon baking soda
- 1/2 teaspoon baking powder
- 1/2 teaspoon salt
- 1 teaspoon ground cinnamon
- 1/2 teaspoon ground nutmeg
- 1/4 teaspoon ground cloves
- 1/4 teaspoon ground ginger
- 1/2 cup unsalted butter, softened
- 1 cup granulated sugar
- 2 large eggs
- 1 cup pumpkin puree
- 1/4 cup milk
- 1 teaspoon vanilla extract

Instructions:

1. Preheat your oven to 350°F (175°C). Grease and flour a 9x5-inch loaf pan.
2. In a medium bowl, whisk together the flour, baking soda, baking powder, salt, cinnamon, nutmeg, cloves, and ginger until well combined. Set aside.
3. In a large mixing bowl, cream together the softened butter and granulated sugar until light and fluffy.
4. Beat in the eggs, one at a time, until well combined. Then, mix in the pumpkin puree, milk, and vanilla extract until smooth.
5. Gradually add the dry ingredients to the wet ingredients, mixing until just combined. Be careful not to overmix.
6. Pour the batter into the prepared loaf pan, spreading it out evenly.
7. Bake in the preheated oven for 50-60 minutes, or until a toothpick inserted into the center comes out clean.
8. Remove the pumpkin bread from the oven and allow it to cool in the pan for about 10 minutes before transferring it to a wire rack to cool completely.
9. Once cooled, slice the pumpkin bread and serve.

10. Enjoy your homemade Pumpkin Bread as a delicious and moist treat, perfect for autumn!

Feel free to add chopped nuts or chocolate chips to the batter for extra flavor and texture. You can also sprinkle some cinnamon sugar on top of the bread before baking for a sweet and crunchy crust.

Sweet Red Bean Milk Bread (팥빵): Soft and fluffy milk bread filled with sweet red bean paste, a classic Korean bakery treat.

Ingredients:

For the Milk Bread Dough:

- 2 1/2 cups bread flour
- 1/4 cup granulated sugar
- 1 teaspoon salt
- 2 teaspoons instant yeast
- 1/2 cup warm milk
- 1/4 cup unsalted butter, melted
- 1 large egg

For the Filling:

- 1 cup sweet red bean paste (store-bought or homemade)

Instructions:

1. In a large mixing bowl, combine the bread flour, sugar, salt, and instant yeast.
2. In a separate bowl, whisk together the warm milk, melted butter, and egg.
3. Pour the wet ingredients into the dry ingredients and mix until a dough forms.
4. Knead the dough on a lightly floured surface for about 5-7 minutes until it becomes smooth and elastic.
5. Place the dough in a greased bowl, cover it with a clean kitchen towel, and let it rise in a warm place for about 1-2 hours until it doubles in size.
6. Once the dough has risen, punch it down and divide it into equal-sized portions.
7. Flatten each portion of dough into a small circle.
8. Spoon a dollop of sweet red bean paste onto the center of each dough circle.
9. Carefully gather the edges of the dough up and around the filling, pinching them together to seal and form a bread roll.
10. Place the stuffed bread rolls on a baking sheet lined with parchment paper, leaving some space between each roll.
11. Cover the rolls loosely with a clean kitchen towel and let them rise for another 30-45 minutes.

12. Preheat your oven to 350°F (175°C).
13. Once the rolls have risen, bake them in the preheated oven for 15-20 minutes until they are golden brown and cooked through.
14. Remove the rolls from the oven and let them cool slightly before serving.
15. Enjoy your homemade Sweet Red Bean Milk Bread warm as a delicious and classic Korean bakery treat!

Feel free to brush the tops of the rolls with a beaten egg wash before baking for a shiny finish. You can also sprinkle some sesame seeds on top of the rolls for added flavor and decoration.

Cream Cheese Walnut Bread (크림치즈 호두빵): Bread rolls filled with creamy cheese and crunchy walnuts, offering a delightful combination of flavors and textures.

Ingredients:

For the Bread Dough:

- 3 cups all-purpose flour
- 1/4 cup granulated sugar
- 1 teaspoon salt
- 2 teaspoons instant yeast
- 1 cup warm milk
- 1/4 cup unsalted butter, melted
- 1 large egg

For the Filling:

- 1/2 cup cream cheese, softened
- 1/2 cup chopped walnuts
- 1/4 cup granulated sugar
- 1 teaspoon vanilla extract

Instructions:

1. In a large mixing bowl, combine the flour, sugar, salt, and instant yeast.
2. In a separate bowl, whisk together the warm milk, melted butter, and egg.
3. Pour the wet ingredients into the dry ingredients and mix until a dough forms.
4. Knead the dough on a lightly floured surface for about 5-7 minutes until it becomes smooth and elastic.
5. Place the dough in a greased bowl, cover it with a clean kitchen towel, and let it rise in a warm place for about 1-2 hours until it doubles in size.
6. Meanwhile, prepare the filling. In a mixing bowl, combine the softened cream cheese, chopped walnuts, granulated sugar, and vanilla extract until well combined.
7. Once the dough has risen, punch it down and divide it into equal-sized portions.

8. Flatten each portion of dough into a small circle.
9. Spoon a generous amount of the cream cheese and walnut filling onto the center of each dough circle.
10. Carefully gather the edges of the dough up and around the filling, pinching them together to seal and form a bread roll.
11. Place the stuffed bread rolls on a baking sheet lined with parchment paper, leaving some space between each roll.
12. Cover the rolls loosely with a clean kitchen towel and let them rise for another 30-45 minutes.
13. Preheat your oven to 350°F (175°C).
14. Once the rolls have risen, bake them in the preheated oven for 20-25 minutes until they are golden brown and cooked through.
15. Remove the rolls from the oven and let them cool slightly before serving.
16. Enjoy your homemade Cream Cheese Walnut Bread warm as a delicious and flavorful treat!

Feel free to add a sprinkle of powdered sugar on top of the rolls for added sweetness before serving. You can also drizzle some honey over the rolls for an extra touch of sweetness.

Honey Almond Bread (꿀 아몬드빵): Bread rolls drizzled with honey and topped with sliced almonds, offering a sweet and nutty flavor.

Ingredients:

For the Bread Dough:

- 3 cups all-purpose flour
- 1/4 cup granulated sugar
- 1 teaspoon salt
- 2 teaspoons instant yeast
- 1 cup warm milk
- 1/4 cup unsalted butter, melted
- 1 large egg

For Topping:

- Honey, for drizzling
- Sliced almonds, for sprinkling

Instructions:

1. In a large mixing bowl, combine the flour, sugar, salt, and instant yeast.
2. In a separate bowl, whisk together the warm milk, melted butter, and egg.
3. Pour the wet ingredients into the dry ingredients and mix until a dough forms.
4. Knead the dough on a lightly floured surface for about 5-7 minutes until it becomes smooth and elastic.
5. Place the dough in a greased bowl, cover it with a clean kitchen towel, and let it rise in a warm place for about 1-2 hours until it doubles in size.
6. Once the dough has risen, punch it down and divide it into equal-sized portions.
7. Shape each portion of dough into a small ball and place them on a baking sheet lined with parchment paper, leaving some space between each roll.
8. Cover the rolls loosely with a clean kitchen towel and let them rise for another 30-45 minutes.
9. Preheat your oven to 350°F (175°C).

10. Once the rolls have risen, bake them in the preheated oven for 15-20 minutes until they are golden brown and cooked through.
11. Remove the rolls from the oven and let them cool slightly.
12. Drizzle honey over the warm rolls and sprinkle sliced almonds on top.
13. Serve your homemade Honey Almond Bread warm as a delicious and sweet treat!

Feel free to brush the tops of the rolls with melted butter before baking for added richness. You can also sprinkle some cinnamon on top of the rolls along with the sliced almonds for extra flavor.

Green Tea Red Bean Bread (녹차 팥빵): Bread rolls infused with green tea flavor and filled with sweet red bean paste, offering a unique and delicious taste.

Ingredients:

For the Green Tea Bread Dough:

- 2 1/2 cups bread flour
- 1/4 cup granulated sugar
- 1 teaspoon salt
- 2 teaspoons instant yeast
- 1/2 cup warm milk
- 1/4 cup unsalted butter, melted
- 1 large egg
- 2 tablespoons matcha green tea powder

For the Filling:

- 1 cup sweet red bean paste (store-bought or homemade)

Instructions:

1. In a large mixing bowl, combine the bread flour, sugar, salt, instant yeast, and matcha green tea powder.
2. In a separate bowl, whisk together the warm milk, melted butter, and egg.
3. Pour the wet ingredients into the dry ingredients and mix until a dough forms.
4. Knead the dough on a lightly floured surface for about 5-7 minutes until it becomes smooth and elastic.
5. Place the dough in a greased bowl, cover it with a clean kitchen towel, and let it rise in a warm place for about 1-2 hours until it doubles in size.
6. Once the dough has risen, punch it down and divide it into equal-sized portions.
7. Flatten each portion of dough into a small circle.
8. Spoon a dollop of sweet red bean paste onto the center of each dough circle.
9. Carefully gather the edges of the dough up and around the filling, pinching them together to seal and form a bread roll.

10. Place the stuffed bread rolls on a baking sheet lined with parchment paper, leaving some space between each roll.
11. Cover the rolls loosely with a clean kitchen towel and let them rise for another 30-45 minutes.
12. Preheat your oven to 350°F (175°C).
13. Once the rolls have risen, bake them in the preheated oven for 15-20 minutes until they are golden brown and cooked through.
14. Remove the rolls from the oven and let them cool slightly before serving.
15. Enjoy your homemade Green Tea Red Bean Bread warm as a delicious and unique treat!

Feel free to sprinkle some sesame seeds on top of the rolls before baking for added flavor and decoration. You can also brush the tops of the rolls with a beaten egg wash for a shiny finish.

Sweet Potato Chestnut Bread (고구마 밤빵): Bread made with mashed sweet potatoes and studded with chestnuts, offering a sweet and nutty flavor profile.

Ingredients:

- 2 cups all-purpose flour
- 1/2 cup granulated sugar
- 1 teaspoon baking powder
- 1/2 teaspoon baking soda
- 1/4 teaspoon salt
- 1 teaspoon ground cinnamon
- 1/2 teaspoon ground nutmeg
- 1/4 teaspoon ground cloves
- 1/4 teaspoon ground ginger
- 1 cup mashed sweet potatoes (cooked and cooled)
- 1/2 cup vegetable oil
- 2 large eggs
- 1/4 cup milk
- 1 teaspoon vanilla extract
- 1 cup chopped chestnuts

Instructions:

1. Preheat your oven to 350°F (175°C). Grease and flour a 9x5-inch loaf pan.
2. In a large mixing bowl, whisk together the flour, sugar, baking powder, baking soda, salt, cinnamon, nutmeg, cloves, and ginger until well combined.
3. In a separate bowl, mix together the mashed sweet potatoes, vegetable oil, eggs, milk, and vanilla extract until smooth.
4. Pour the wet ingredients into the dry ingredients and stir until just combined. Do not overmix.
5. Gently fold in the chopped chestnuts until evenly distributed throughout the batter.
6. Pour the batter into the prepared loaf pan and spread it out evenly.
7. Bake in the preheated oven for 50-60 minutes, or until a toothpick inserted into the center comes out clean.
8. Remove the bread from the oven and allow it to cool in the pan for 10 minutes before transferring it to a wire rack to cool completely.

9. Once cooled, slice the Sweet Potato Chestnut Bread and serve.
10. Enjoy your homemade Sweet Potato Chestnut Bread as a delicious and flavorful treat!

Feel free to add a sprinkle of powdered sugar on top of the bread before serving for extra sweetness. You can also toast the slices of bread and serve them with butter for a delightful snack.

Sesame Seed Sweet Bread (참깨 단빵): Sweet bread rolls coated with sesame seeds for a nutty flavor and crunchy texture.

Ingredients:

For the Bread Dough:

- 3 cups all-purpose flour
- 1/4 cup granulated sugar
- 1 teaspoon salt
- 2 teaspoons instant yeast
- 1 cup warm milk
- 1/4 cup unsalted butter, melted
- 1 large egg

For Topping:

- Sesame seeds
- Honey or syrup (optional)

Instructions:

1. In a large mixing bowl, combine the flour, sugar, salt, and instant yeast.
2. In a separate bowl, whisk together the warm milk, melted butter, and egg.
3. Pour the wet ingredients into the dry ingredients and mix until a dough forms.
4. Knead the dough on a lightly floured surface for about 5-7 minutes until it becomes smooth and elastic.
5. Place the dough in a greased bowl, cover it with a clean kitchen towel, and let it rise in a warm place for about 1-2 hours until it doubles in size.
6. Once the dough has risen, punch it down and divide it into equal-sized portions.
7. Shape each portion of dough into a small ball.
8. Roll each ball of dough in sesame seeds, making sure to coat the entire surface.
9. Place the sesame seed-coated bread rolls on a baking sheet lined with parchment paper, leaving some space between each roll.

10. Cover the rolls loosely with a clean kitchen towel and let them rise for another 30-45 minutes.
11. Preheat your oven to 350°F (175°C).
12. Once the rolls have risen, bake them in the preheated oven for 15-20 minutes until they are golden brown and cooked through.
13. Remove the rolls from the oven and let them cool slightly.
14. Optionally, drizzle honey or syrup over the warm rolls for added sweetness.
15. Serve your homemade Sesame Seed Sweet Bread warm as a delicious and crunchy treat!

Feel free to customize the sweetness of the bread by adjusting the amount of sugar in the dough or by adding more honey or syrup on top. You can also experiment with different types of sesame seeds, such as black sesame seeds, for a unique flavor and appearance.

Cream Corn Milk Bread (크림 옥수수우유빵): Soft milk bread rolls filled with creamy sweet corn filling, offering a sweet and comforting taste.

Ingredients:

For the Bread Dough:

- 3 cups bread flour
- 1/4 cup granulated sugar
- 1 teaspoon salt
- 2 teaspoons instant yeast
- 1/2 cup warm milk
- 1/4 cup unsalted butter, melted
- 1 large egg

For the Cream Corn Filling:

- 1 cup canned cream-style corn
- 1/4 cup granulated sugar
- 2 tablespoons all-purpose flour
- 1/4 cup milk

Instructions:

1. In a large mixing bowl, combine the bread flour, sugar, salt, and instant yeast.
2. In a separate bowl, whisk together the warm milk, melted butter, and egg.
3. Pour the wet ingredients into the dry ingredients and mix until a dough forms.
4. Knead the dough on a lightly floured surface for about 5-7 minutes until it becomes smooth and elastic.
5. Place the dough in a greased bowl, cover it with a clean kitchen towel, and let it rise in a warm place for about 1-2 hours until it doubles in size.
6. Meanwhile, prepare the cream corn filling. In a saucepan, combine the cream-style corn, sugar, all-purpose flour, and milk. Cook over medium heat, stirring constantly, until the mixture thickens. Remove from heat and let it cool.
7. Once the dough has risen, punch it down and divide it into equal-sized portions.

8. Flatten each portion of dough into a small circle.
9. Spoon a dollop of the cream corn filling onto the center of each dough circle.
10. Carefully gather the edges of the dough up and around the filling, pinching them together to seal and form a bread roll.
11. Place the stuffed bread rolls on a baking sheet lined with parchment paper, leaving some space between each roll.
12. Cover the rolls loosely with a clean kitchen towel and let them rise for another 30-45 minutes.
13. Preheat your oven to 350°F (175°C).
14. Once the rolls have risen, bake them in the preheated oven for 15-20 minutes until they are golden brown and cooked through.
15. Remove the rolls from the oven and let them cool slightly before serving.
16. Enjoy your homemade Cream Corn Milk Bread warm as a delicious and comforting treat!

Feel free to sprinkle some shredded cheese on top of the cream corn filling before sealing the rolls for added flavor. You can also brush the tops of the rolls with melted butter before baking for a shiny finish.

Chocolate Cream Bread (초콜릿 크림빵): Soft bread rolls filled with rich chocolate cream filling, perfect for chocolate lovers.

Ingredients:

For the Bread Dough:

- 3 cups bread flour
- 1/4 cup granulated sugar
- 1 teaspoon salt
- 2 teaspoons instant yeast
- 1/2 cup warm milk
- 1/4 cup unsalted butter, melted
- 1 large egg

For the Chocolate Cream Filling:

- 1 cup heavy cream
- 1 cup semisweet chocolate chips
- 2 tablespoons unsalted butter
- 2 tablespoons powdered sugar
- 1 teaspoon vanilla extract

Instructions:

1. In a large mixing bowl, combine the bread flour, sugar, salt, and instant yeast.
2. In a separate bowl, whisk together the warm milk, melted butter, and egg.
3. Pour the wet ingredients into the dry ingredients and mix until a dough forms.
4. Knead the dough on a lightly floured surface for about 5-7 minutes until it becomes smooth and elastic.
5. Place the dough in a greased bowl, cover it with a clean kitchen towel, and let it rise in a warm place for about 1-2 hours until it doubles in size.
6. Meanwhile, prepare the chocolate cream filling. In a saucepan, heat the heavy cream over medium heat until it just begins to simmer.

7. Remove the cream from the heat and add the chocolate chips and butter. Let it sit for a few minutes, then stir until the chocolate is completely melted and the mixture is smooth.
8. Stir in the powdered sugar and vanilla extract until well combined. Let the chocolate cream filling cool to room temperature.
9. Once the dough has risen, punch it down and divide it into equal-sized portions.
10. Flatten each portion of dough into a small circle.
11. Spoon a dollop of the chocolate cream filling onto the center of each dough circle.
12. Carefully gather the edges of the dough up and around the filling, pinching them together to seal and form a bread roll.
13. Place the stuffed bread rolls on a baking sheet lined with parchment paper, leaving some space between each roll.
14. Cover the rolls loosely with a clean kitchen towel and let them rise for another 30-45 minutes.
15. Preheat your oven to 350°F (175°C).
16. Once the rolls have risen, bake them in the preheated oven for 15-20 minutes until they are golden brown and cooked through.
17. Remove the rolls from the oven and let them cool slightly before serving.
18. Enjoy your homemade Chocolate Cream Bread warm as a decadent and indulgent treat!

Feel free to dust the tops of the rolls with powdered sugar or cocoa powder before serving for added presentation. You can also sprinkle some chocolate chips on top of the rolls before baking for extra chocolatey goodness.

Green Onion Cheese Bread (파 치즈빵): Bread rolls filled with melted cheese and chopped green onions, offering a savory and flavorful taste.

Ingredients:

For the Bread Dough:

- 3 cups bread flour
- 1/4 cup granulated sugar
- 1 teaspoon salt
- 2 teaspoons instant yeast
- 1/2 cup warm milk
- 1/4 cup unsalted butter, melted
- 1 large egg

For the Filling:

- 1 1/2 cups shredded cheese (such as cheddar or mozzarella)
- 1/2 cup chopped green onions

Instructions:

1. In a large mixing bowl, combine the bread flour, sugar, salt, and instant yeast.
2. In a separate bowl, whisk together the warm milk, melted butter, and egg.
3. Pour the wet ingredients into the dry ingredients and mix until a dough forms.
4. Knead the dough on a lightly floured surface for about 5-7 minutes until it becomes smooth and elastic.
5. Place the dough in a greased bowl, cover it with a clean kitchen towel, and let it rise in a warm place for about 1-2 hours until it doubles in size.
6. Once the dough has risen, punch it down and divide it into equal-sized portions.
7. Flatten each portion of dough into a small circle.
8. Sprinkle some shredded cheese and chopped green onions onto the center of each dough circle.
9. Carefully gather the edges of the dough up and around the filling, pinching them together to seal and form a bread roll.

10. Place the stuffed bread rolls on a baking sheet lined with parchment paper, leaving some space between each roll.
11. Cover the rolls loosely with a clean kitchen towel and let them rise for another 30-45 minutes.
12. Preheat your oven to 350°F (175°C).
13. Once the rolls have risen, bake them in the preheated oven for 15-20 minutes until they are golden brown and the cheese is melted and bubbly.
14. Remove the rolls from the oven and let them cool slightly before serving.
15. Enjoy your homemade Green Onion Cheese Bread warm as a savory and flavorful snack or side dish!

Feel free to customize the filling by adding other ingredients such as cooked bacon, ham, or jalapenos for added flavor. You can also brush the tops of the rolls with melted butter and sprinkle some garlic powder or herbs for extra flavor.

Sweet Red Bean Twist Bread (팥빵): Twisted bread rolls filled with sweet red bean paste, offering a fun and delicious treat.

Ingredients:

For the Dough:

- 3 cups all-purpose flour
- 1/4 cup granulated sugar
- 1 teaspoon salt
- 2 teaspoons instant yeast
- 1 cup warm milk
- 1/4 cup unsalted butter, melted
- 1 large egg

For the Filling:

- 1 cup sweet red bean paste (store-bought or homemade)

For Egg Wash:

- 1 large egg, beaten
- 1 tablespoon milk

Instructions:

1. In a large mixing bowl, combine the flour, sugar, salt, and instant yeast.
2. In a separate bowl, whisk together the warm milk, melted butter, and egg.
3. Pour the wet ingredients into the dry ingredients and mix until a dough forms.
4. Knead the dough on a lightly floured surface for about 5-7 minutes until it becomes smooth and elastic.
5. Place the dough in a greased bowl, cover it with a clean kitchen towel, and let it rise in a warm place for about 1-2 hours until it doubles in size.
6. Once the dough has risen, punch it down and divide it into equal-sized portions.

7. Roll each portion of dough into a long rope about 12 inches in length.
8. Flatten each rope slightly and spread a tablespoon of sweet red bean paste along the length of the rope.
9. Fold the dough over the filling and pinch the edges to seal.
10. Twist the filled dough ropes gently and shape them into a spiral.
11. Place the twisted bread rolls on a baking sheet lined with parchment paper, leaving some space between each roll.
12. Cover the rolls loosely with a clean kitchen towel and let them rise for another 30-45 minutes.
13. Preheat your oven to 350°F (175°C).
14. In a small bowl, beat together the egg and milk to make the egg wash.
15. Brush the tops of the risen rolls with the egg wash.
16. Bake the rolls in the preheated oven for 15-20 minutes until they are golden brown and cooked through.
17. Remove the rolls from the oven and let them cool slightly before serving.
18. Enjoy your homemade Sweet Red Bean Twist Bread warm as a delicious and fun treat!

Feel free to sprinkle some sesame seeds or powdered sugar on top of the rolls before baking for added flavor and decoration.

www.ingramcontent.com/pod-product-compliance
Lightning Source LLC
LaVergne TN
LVHW081601060526
838201LV00054B/2012